Designs for Garden Paths

150 Designs
for Walkways,
Terraces and Steps

Heidi Howcroft

4880 Lower Valley Road, Atglen, PA 19310 USA

Acknowledgments

Paving would never have gained the significance it now has for me without my direct contact with contractors and especially master paviors. I would like to thank all those who have advised and supported me throughout the years, above all Bernhard Kroiß, Peter and Binette Nickl, my assistant Katrin Schulze, and also my brother Peter Howcroft who has accompanied me on many a paving tour.

Special thanks are due to the Vereinigten Granit Betrieben Fürstenstein, Germany, whose sample panels photographed by George Meister appear in this book. Finally, thanks to my German publishers Callwey Verlag, in particular Roland Thomas, Andrea Hölzl, and Dorothea Montigel.

Howcroft, Heidi.
    [Pflaster im Garten, English]
    Designs for garden paths: 150 designs for walkways, terraces, and steps/Heidi Howcroft.
        p. cm.
    Translation of: Pflaster im Garten.
    ISBN 0-7643-0383-X (hardcover)
    1. Garden walks--Designs and plans. I. Title.
TH4970.H63   1997
712'.6--dc21   97-22420
                    CIP

Copyright © 1997 by Schiffer Publishing Ltd.
Originally published by Georg D. W. Callwey GmbH & Co., Streitfeldstrasse 35, 81673 Munich, Germany

ISBN: 0-7643-0383-X
Printed in Hong Kong

Published by Schiffer Publishing Ltd.
4880 Lower Valley Road
Atglen, PA 19310
Phone: (610) 593-1777; Fax: (610) 593-2002
E-mail: Schifferbk@aol.com
Please write for a free catalog.
This book may be purchased from the publisher.
Please include $3.95 for shipping.

In Europe, Schiffer books are distributed by
Bushwood Books
84 Bushwood Lane
Kew Gardens
Surrey TW9 3BQ England
Phone: 44 (0)181 948-8119; Fax: 44 (0)181 948-3232
E-mail: Bushwd@aol.com

Please try your bookstore first.

We are interested in hearing from authors with book ideas on related subjects.

[Endpapers]

An unusual but highly effective combination of bright blue ceramic spheres and pebbles.

The surface underfoot highlights the transition from one garden room to another; a grass path at the entrance, followed by a brick surface, returning to grass in the adjoining room.

Mixing materials can be
exciting and can enrich
the surface, emphasizing
the character of each
individual material.

Contents

Introduction

Gardens are often considered simply in terms of their planting. Gardeners and designers can be understandably preoccupied with planning exciting combinations of plants and searching for species that provide interest and color contrast, while paying little attention to the design potential of the garden's hard surfaces.

Lack of interest, lack of awareness, lack of knowledge, or timidity are additional reasons why this subject is neglected. It is often regarded as a mere necessity to surface a path or pave a terrace.

But paving is far more than just a floor cover. It influences the appearance of the whole garden, and at its best creates interest all year round through the quality of the design. Paving is usually the most expensive aspect of the garden and cannot be changed at a whim. Good examples obviously lie flat on the ground, so unless you are given to peeping over garden fences you must rely on books, magazines, and garden centers for inspiration. Unfortunately, garden centers can display only a limited range of materials, while books and magazines tend to concentrate on attractive planting rather than paving. Design ideas and technical data from specialized manufacturers tend to be directed at professional designers and seldom filter down to the layperson.

This book seeks to fill this information gap in an interesting and informative manner. It illustrates the wide range of materials and techniques available, using carefully selected examples photographed by internationally renown photographers, supplemented by technical drawings. The book also attempts to correct the myth that all paving is expensive. Although based largely on German practice, *Designs for Garden Paths* also explores examples from other cultures. The result is a practical sourcebook intended to generate and inspire ideas for your own garden.

Throughout the book, the term "paving" has been deliberately used in its broadest sense to include not only traditional paving but all types of surfaces from loose aggregates to grass paths. Paving is a fascinating subject. Developing an awareness of well-laid surfaces that complement buildings and their surroundings enhances one's appreciation of quality paving and beautiful gardens. Once you are hooked, a whole new world will open up!

Heidi Howcroft, Munich 1997

Without paving a garden
is not complete. Even in
its simplest form, when
properly chosen and
executed, paving is an
important part of the
garden.

Hard Surfaces in the Garden

Just how much of the garden is covered with paving is often not understood. Only when all hard surfaces, including the garage entrance, the area around the house, and all the paths, are added together does it become apparent how large the area truly is. Designated as purely functional and thus generally ignored, these areas should not be left to chance but rather given as much thought as any other part of the garden. At the turn of the century it was considered quite normal to enhance a beautiful garden with equally beautiful paving material. Today, more and more people are becoming aware of this link. Gardens and hard surfaces belong together. Paving can exude an air of quality, be it a simple background to a flower bed, or a rich ornamental floorscape.

The assortment of hard surfaces shown in this book ranges from classic gravel surfaces, timber in all its forms, and innovative concrete paving to functional brick paving, carefully laid mosaic pebbles, and the full scope of traditional stone. The examples illustrate that a path is more than just a route, a terrace more than just a platform for furniture. All are important parts of the garden deserving more attention than they often receive.

A roundel of large natural paving stones surrounding a geometrically cut millstone marks the junction of several paths. In a well thought-out design individual features can be highlighted using paving.

This well known scene from the Barnsley House Gardens demonstrates the parallels between interior decorating and garden design. Ceiling and walls are formed by the laburnum arch. The floor covering is a rug of alternately dark and white pebbles between broad slabs making the path appear narrower and emphasizing the length and focal point.

Paths - the Backbone of the Garden

Generally regarded as merely useful and functional, a garden path is not just a link between two points and a method of getting around without soiling one's shoes. Paths are an essential element of garden design, providing the backbone of the garden without which the garden cannot be enjoyed. They are both guidelines and divisions. When seen from above, they appear to be brush strokes, lines which give the garden structure. Since paths are situated between or adjacent to areas of interest, very little attention is usually paid to them.

The type of hard surface and how it is laid influences the whole atmosphere of the garden. Is the path straight as a ramrod or gently curved, what color is its surface, how is it textured, does it lead to a focal point? All of these are important considerations. Details are just as important as the overall design; what is the point of creating a beautiful flower bed if the color of the adjoining path ruins the composition?

A well designed network of paths can make a small garden appear larger and can pull a large garden together, giving it structure and ordering the spaces so they seem contained. Using false perspectives and the right material laid in an appropriate pattern can even make a long path appear shorter or a short path wider.

Until the introduction of the landscape garden in the nineteenth century, garden paths were rigid and straight in accordance with the design of the period. The serpentine path, a wandering, meandering path developed from the formal S-path, was an important element in the landscape garden, a break from formal convention. Freed from geometric constraints, the garden became at one with nature. No garden, not even the smallest, was without promenades - a network of criss-crossing winding paths that penetrated the furthest corners of the garden. Today we do not understand the historical importance of paths and how they constituted a major design feature. Contemporary gardens might be free of fashion dogma - all styles, even combinations of styles are permitted - but the path as a design statement is sadly neglected.

Regardless of the path's location, a clear hierarchy determined by function and frequency of use must be established. The main path is similar to the main artery. Even in the tiniest garden two people should be able to walk side by side. A minimum width of 3 feet, 6 inches is recommended. The maximum width in large gardens, where the path may double as a drive, is 10 feet. Any wider and the path becomes more like a roadway. One tip, taken from old French garden design and very useful in large gardens, is that a path´s width should be proportional to its length: the longer the path the wider it should be, thus camouflaging the true length. In the handkerchief-sized plots of today, the opposite is often the case. Efforts are made to stretch the central path and the garden to make them seem larger than they really are. A trick frequently used in designs is to use small sized or long, thin paving elements laid at a right angle to the direction of the path in order to stress the width. Of all paths the main one must be edged, both for structural reasons and to emphasize its importance.

Branching off from the main path are the secondary paths, which should be noticeably narrower. Two thirds the width of the main path is a good rule of thumb. While both the main and secondary paths can be laid in the same material, the subordinate paths should not be over-designed. The lowest grade of paths are those peeling off the main or secondary routes through plant beds or into the far corners of the garden. They are without any sort of edging and no pretense of design, often just the width of a paving slab and intended to provide access for a wheel-barrow.

Daring and successful,
this winding path in
basket weave dominates
the long narrow terrace
garden.

Just how different two
paths of identical width
can appear is illustrated
in these photographs.

Right: Stone slabs have
been removed at irregu-
lar intervals and re-
placed by planting. The
edges are softened and
the path itself becomes
narrower but has not lost
any of its importance.

Below: A wide formal
flagstone path, flanked
by lavender, leads
straight to the opening in
the wall. The eye is
drawn automatically to
the doorway, which may
in fact be only a side
entrance.

Opposite page: Many
details from the York
Gate Garden can also be
used in much smaller
gardens. The design of
the main path, which is
laid out in paving stone
diamonds fringed by an

edging in the same
material and with loose
gravel in-between, has
the effect of relating the
roundel in the path to the
round window at the
vista's end.

While a 10' wide main path (left) is fitting for a stately home, the 5´ width shown below is more suitable for a private garden. The lightly curved gravel path links one part of the garden with the other.

Left: Nestled between sorrel beds framed with lavender is a narrow gravel path. The color of the gravel comes from the rock type, in this case a golden Cotswolds limestone.

The way in which
these slabs are laid
in combination with
other materials
elevates an other-
wise insignificant
secondary path into
a major design
element. Individually
inscribed slabs set
like precious
diamonds in grass
lead to a focal point.
In Ian Hamilton
Finlay´s garden, the
path assumes a far
greater significance
than merely a route.

Instead of being laid lengthwise, these pebbles are packed tightly together like eggs. They are not to be walked on, but purely to be admired.

Beaten tracks are for explorers. Loved by children and adults alike, they are traces of human activity, created by trampling over the same piece of earth time and time again. The childhood memory of weeding formal gravel paths was so vivid for the director of a Viennese art gallery that upon inheriting the family house and garden she immediately let all paths become overgrown and simply allowed a network of ever changing tracks to run through the plot. The formality of paths was dispensed with, the freedom of walking and exploring encouraged.

At the other end of the scale are ornamental paths, never intended for actual use but provided solely for the visual enhancement of the garden. They are an essential component of parterres in renaissance gardens, little more than ground cover consisting of white, pink, black, or green bands of gravel flanked by box hedges.

If a path needs to be concealed, it is possible to use a design element developed in English landscape gardens to hide it from view. The theory is that if the path lies lower than its surroundings - in a type of ditch, for example - it will appear from a distance as if nothing interrupts the flow of the landscape. The wider the path the deeper the ditch must be. This design idea is especially useful in large gardens laid with grass.

The width of a path
depends on its
frequency of use:
the more it is used
the wider it becomes
and more dominant
it is in the garden.

Left: This track is a
shortcut between
two formal paths. It
is used so much that
instead of being left
as bare earth it has
been covered with
crushed stone.

As shown in the
middle photograph,
paths which are
seldom used take on
the appearance of
tracks after a while.
The plants here have
invaded the path,
their soft edges
complementing the
romantic flower
garden.

Right: The 1' 6" gap
left free between the
rows of plant pots is
sufficient as an
access path.

The ultimate planted path. Barely a trace of the once broad path remains between the helianthemums.

Color and direction: this photograph captures the fleeting culmination of this design. The line of the path is reinforced by the fortuitous effect of the fallen laburnum blossom.

The Front Garden

Between the garden gate and front door lies the most neglected area in the whole garden. The front garden is in the limelight, a visiting card for the house and owners. Marble floors and exquisite decor might proliferate inside, but they are not visible to the outsider, only the front garden is. This is not the place for cost cutting. If money must be saved, do so in the back garden, not in this sensitive spot. At the same time the front area should not be "kitschy." A pot-pourri of checked patterns or highly polished stone (which has more in common with a cemetery than a front yard), should be avoided. An impressive balanced design is both needed and appropriate here.

Below: Generous and inviting, the wide low natural stone steps stretch from the garden gate to the front door.

Often the design of the front garden is the most difficult. If you have restricted space you could, for example, combine the parking space and entrance. Using a good surface material the piazza-like courtyard shown above also works well as an approach to the house.

Right: A distinctive line leading to the front door solves the problem of an entrance which is set back and hidden.

Even the smallest area can be designed. Here are three variations, all conveying a personal touch.

Top: A natural stone slab as a doormat, framed by brown pebbles, renders a demarcation of private space. The step in front of the front door is indicated by a single row of dark pebbles. Middle: This tread is decorated with a star, declaring it to be something special. Bottom: Diagonally laid pebbles point to the entrance.

Decorative patterns at the entrance are like a visiting card, setting the tone for what lies inside. The design possibilities of ornamental paving are inexhaustible and offer something different for everyone.

The Building Perimeter

Originally introduced as a necessary protective strip, laid in rubble stone or paving slabs directly against the plinth of the house, the building perimeter is basically just a strip of paving and is just as important today as ever. As in the past, this strip protects the facade from any type of moisture. It has a minimum width of 18 inches. From a design point of view, the paving strip forms a clean base around the building, a transition between what is built and what is planted. The house appears to grow out of the paving. Unfortunately, this area is frequently treated as a "no-man's-land": a lifeless dull gravel channel, functional but without any thought for appearance, light years away from historical examples, which at their peak resembled piazza paving. The material used need not be expensive, only suitable and harmonious with the style of the house and surroundings. Innumerable ideas including small element paving stones, brick, or the most simple of concrete units can enhance this area. The paving should always be laid with a slant away from the building, so that surface water can run off. Living conditions for plants are poor beneath the eaves. Once out of the dry covered zone, plant pockets can be incorporated in the paving to add an element of green.

The Garage Entrance

A necessity and yet seemingly a waste of valuable garden space, the garage entrance is another neglected area. A parking place sometimes hidden, sometimes visible, it is a part of the garden without any outstanding "gardenesque" qualities. As one of the largest hard surface areas in the garden (generally at least 160 square feet) it can, if properly treated, be a quite interesting area. Bearing in mind practical considerations, such as surface water drainage, adequate base construction for the anticipated load, and correct size of material and laying, the square or rectangular areas can be well designed. Simple features like a frame of decorative paving stones lifts the area from ordinary to special. For a more natural look, the edges can be softened and even have grass joints. Sometimes an unavoidable number of manhole covers, gullies and the like congregate in this area; by framing them with a row of stones all can be smoothly integrated into the surface.

Terraces and Patios

A house without a terrace is like a dog without an owner, both seem lost. Everyone enjoys sitting outside, eating "al fresco." Large enough for a table and chairs, this highly valued outdoor room is really an extension of the house. What would summer be like without a pleasant hour or two spent on the terrace or patio?

Once the basic considerations regarding location, size and relationship to the garden as a whole have been made, one must consider the details. Is the area really large enough for the garden furniture? How should the relationship to the neighboring areas be made? Which surface material should be used ? New houses tend to have very tight, almost Lilliputian sized terraces, with just enough room for a minuscule table and two chairs. In order to fully enjoy the outdoor feeling sufficient space is needed; this indicates that an extension may be necessary. It is of course preferable to be generous from the start. The terrace need not have the dimensions of a ballroom, but must reflect the size of the family and their hospitality.

Unfortunately, not all parts of the country enjoy the benefits of a Mediterranean-type climate. During many months of the year the terrace surface lies empty and appears forlorn

if nothing is done for the winter picture. Admittedly when covered with a blanket of snow everything appears brighter and friendlier than with the usual greyness. But snow does not lie long, and grey need not be boring. Just a few white marble paving stones can liven up a surface, as can alternating dark and light stones. The paving can either be monochrome or carefully paved in mosaic paving stones like a Persian rug.

As the load bearing requirements rarely extend beyond pedestrian traffic, virtually any material in any pattern variety can be used. The finished surface should be level and stable, suitable for tables and chairs. Wide joints, as well as coarse and uneven stones, are to be avoided.

The terrace should be designed to dry quickly after a shower of rain. Essential requirements for this would be a slant away from the building and a permeable surface and base.

Details and quality of workmanship are important:

• As previously mentioned, covers and gullies must be integrated into the surface. Regardless of which material is used, these elements must be surrounded by a single row of stones or bricks.

• Changes from one bond to another must be marked by a minimum of one row of stones or bricks, which act as a neutral transition.

• Natural stone, concrete, clinker, and brick paving must all be edged.

• Every pattern must be geometrical, clearly visible, and correctly carried out. Even so-called random patterns have a recognizable scheme.

If loose aggregates such as hoggin or gravel are used for patios, regular maintenance is required to keep the appearance. This entails more than just weeding. During hot dry periods it is advisable to hose the area, either in the evening or early morning (so that the water does not evaporate immediately) to reduce dust. Surfaces with grass joints should also be watered. In the interest of water conservation, you may want to restrict watering to those areas most frequently used.

Sitting and Display Areas

Hidden and enclosed sitting areas offer a refuge in the garden, whether in the shade of a tree or in the sun. The surface on which it stands is secondary to the seat itself. Nevertheless, even the smallest area - many are less than 18 square feet - should be in keeping with the garden. Often a simple gravel surface is sufficient. Complicated floorscapes are out of place and cannot be fully appreciated here.

For mobile seats that wander through the garden following the sun, all that is needed are areas with firm and level bases. Grass is ideal.

Sculpture and garden artifacts do need to be prominent. They need a suitable framework and more importantly, a suitable location. The objects should be placed on an appropriate surface a little larger than the object itself, rather like a podium, on which urns, pots, and statues are exhibited. The shape can be taken from the object itself or whatever contrasts best.

The minimum surface area required to accommodate a table and chairs depends on the type of furniture used. Even so, a few guidelines can be provided:

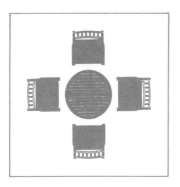

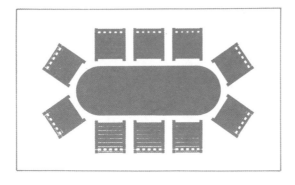

10´ x 10´ for a round table (3' diameter) and four chairs

16´ 6" x 16´ 6" for an oval table with space for ten chairs

12´ 6" x 12´ 6" for a round table (4' diameter) and seven chairs.

Add another 3´ to these minimum sizes to allow for additional furniture such as a barbecue or serving trolley. The golden rule is be as generous as possible with the dimensions.

To enjoy every view and every ray of sunshine the area must be large enough so the bench can swivel in any direction, while ensuring that additional furniture still has space.

This patio has been transformed into a fully furnished outdoor room complete with decorations. Wrapped around the house, it provides an accessible, fully usable, and partly undercover living space.

Typically, the sitting area in many gardens is slightly raised and surrounded by vegetation. Here the low wall acts as rear protection but still allows for a 360° view. The paving as well as the furniture must be in tune with the garden style, as illustrated here by the white filigree metal bench and brick paving.

Left: The transition between the patio and the rest of the garden is elegantly solved by using grass between the stone paving as a bridge. The patio is large enough to enable a multitude of activities. The surface itself is unassuming and functional.

Above: At the end of the garden sits a rustic covered sitting area, a favorite escape even on rainy days. If you look carefully you will notice that the round pattern of the floorcovering is in harmony with the shape of the roof.

In addition to using fixed sitting areas, some people like to wander through the garden searching for sun or shade. All that is required is a level piece of ground and a light comfortable chair or bench.

Garden steps can simply emerge from a lawn. In this case, the risers are made of slim natural stones, set close together and partially covered with rock plants.

Garden Steps

Steps are more than just a practical way of going from one level to another; they are important design features. Whether grand stairways or modest steps, they always attract attention. Steps can be the focal point of the garden, the entrance from which all else radiates, or they can be private and tucked away. Without doubt one of the most difficult garden elements to design and construct, steps must be functional and yet in tune with the overall garden concept. It is easy to be complacent and simply choose the step type from a catalog without any regard to the actual location. The best examples of this can be seen in newly built detached houses. In order to build economically and still include the all important basement, the ground floor is constructed above garden level. Perched even higher, the terrace floats over the garden disconnected from the surrounding space. All variations from hen house ladders to pseudo baroque stairways complete with balustrade have been used in an attempt to link the two levels. Despite all efforts none of these steps looks comfortable or in harmony with their surroundings. By following simple rules, however, a functional and aesthetically pleasing solution is possible.

Basically, the style and orientation of the house indicate where, how, and with what material steps should be constructed. Even so, it is important to differentiate between a formal garden created along strict guidelines and the organic flow of a "natural" or "landscape" garden.

Before reviewing design recommendations for steps, a brief introduction to basic technical terms will help explain the individual components and various types of steps. To begin with, the riser is the vertical section of a step, the tread is the horizontal surface on which one steps, and the stringer is the flanking enclosure of the steps. The relationship between the depth of tread to height of the riser is most important. The proportion must be correct and comfortable. In comparison to steps inside the house, garden steps have wider treads and lower risers. Under no circumstances should interior measurements be applied to the exterior. The calculation is based on a 26 inch stride, using the following rule of thumb:

$$h \text{ (height)} + h + t \text{ (tread)} = 26"$$

All variations are possible, bearing in mind that the minimum riser is 4 inches, the maximum 7 inches. Too high and the steps are uncomfortable and strenuous to climb, too low and they become a hazard.

The best heights are between 5 inches and 6 inches Within a flight of steps the height of each riser must not vary and the number of risers depends on the overall height that must be reached. When calculating the total number of risers required do not forget that a minimum of 2 percent outward fall per tread must be included. A seemingly insignificant figure, this can change the number and height of risers that are required. Work out the total length, as this determines the route and position for the flight of steps. In the case of long flights it can be considerable. There might not be sufficient space to place it parallel to the slope and it may have to be divided into shorter lengths.

The choice of width is not critical but a minimum of 2 feet, 6 inches is recommended. In general it is advisable to be generous with the width, as overhanging vegetation has a narrowing effect. Any surplus space can be used for displaying pots and other garden objects.

Above all, garden steps must be safe. A stable construction prevents steps from wobbling and tipping over. The tread must be nonslip. This is often a problem, particularly with timber. A long flight requires a handrail on both sides; this should not however be misappropriated as a support for plants.

The types of steps described below are classified according to how the treads are constructed. They are suitable for all material and combinations. Paving stones can be used for the tread immediately behind the riser but should never be used as the riser itself.

Right: Steps do not always have to be heavy structures. Sometimes a lighter freestanding construction is more appropriate. In these situations a hand rail is essential even with shorter flights. Here the wooden steps hover over the vegetation heightening the garden experience.

Opposite page: Old limestone steps enriched with lichen and rock plants.

Below: The beginning and the end of each flight of steps is marked symbolically by terracotta urns. A landing punctuates the flights and provides a welcome resting place.

Above: A seemingly endless flight of steps, wide at the bottom and narrower towards the top, disappears into the wood. The secret to the success of this design lies in the consistent use of one material, the adherence to a central axis, and the treatment of the bottom steps.

Functional and without any design pretensions, these solid block steps built into the retaining wall link the lower and upper levels.

Left: The manner in which steps are integrated into their surroundings is very important. Bedded into the meadow, the steps here appear very natural. The overhanging treads give a lightness which is particularly apt.

Below: In woodland gardens steps should appear natural and functional. Wood chippings covering the plant beds flow over into this path. The steps themselves are defined by branches.

Left: Study this example carefully to appreciate the design considerations it illustrates. The deliberate contrast between the light gravel and the dark railway sleepers picks up the strong horizontal element of the pergola. The width of the step itself is in keeping with the surroundings. The proportions between the riser and tread are well chosen.

Block Steps

Built from full blocks of natural stone, concrete, or timber, block steps form a stable and durable all-in-one riser and tread. They are simply built one above the other to form the flight. Wide steps are comprised of several long (generally 3 feet to 5 feet) blocks laid side by side. The block should be laid with a gentle outward fall of 2 - 4 percent to allow surface water to run off. The surface should not be too smooth but rather slightly rough. Natural stone, for example, can be grooved approximately one inch from the front edge to provide a better grip. Concrete steps supplied in lengths of 32 inches to 40 inches and heights of 7 inches are a good alternative to expensive natural stone blocks. A word of caution about railway ties, which were used frequently in the past as garden steps. The proven toxic properties and the slippery surface when wet have virtually banished this recycled product from the garden (refer also to page 98). If safety and durability are valued, natural stone with a slightly roughened tread is the best option. Stone curbs are an interesting and reasonably priced alternative to regular stone blocks.

Tread Slabs

This is a two part construction, comprising a tread slab between 2 inches to 3 1/4 inches in thickness, which rests with a slight overhang (of 2 inches maximum) on blocks. The height of this block construction depends on the total height of the riser. Concrete, brick, and natural stone can all be used. Wonderful examples of this type of garden steps can be seen in historical gardens. This particularly elegant construction is heightened by the shadow cast by the overhang. A good combination is provided by brick risers with stone treads.

Retaining Steps

This is very much a rural or woodland solution. It consists of vertical risers, slabs, or timber boards sunk into the ground behind which the tread is filled or paved. The riser forms a retaining element to contain the tread. Retaining steps are not particularly sturdy and with time the risers, which are generally only rammed into the earth, loosen and lean outwards. For this reason these steps are more suitable in areas where they will only be used occasionally. Another form of these steps are ones using timber posts, depending on the width of the step at each end, with additional supports as necessary, behind which horizontal poles or stems are fixed. Here again the structure weakens with wear and tear and requires regular maintenance. An additional drawback is that the backfilling of the tread can be washed out by rain, leaving just the posts to act as steps - a familiar sight on many a woodland walk.

Step Stiles

This is an uncommon type of step found in combination with drystone walls. Bedded into the wall, the slabs are suspended through 3 inch to 4 inch slabs that protrude from the face of the wall. These steps rarely have more than six treads, graded from largest at the bottom to smallest at the top. These steps are more likely to be for simple access only, having more of a subsidiary function than a main flight of steps.

Landings

Landings or interruptions in a flight of stairs may be necessary for aesthetic reasons to accentuate the stairway and make it a central feature of the garden. More often than not they are there for a technical purpose and to make use of the stairs more comfortable. Long stairways are easier to climb if they are divided at regular intervals by a landing, which can be placed every eight to twelve steps depending on the length of the stairway. The major disadvantage of a straight staircase is the length required to accommodate the combination of steps and landings; in most gardens this length is not available. Instead, the steps must follow the slope, zigzagging to and fro. Changes in direction are only possible with landings, which can take on the form of viewing platforms or resting places equipped with a bench. The width of the landing is the same as for the stairway, its depth depends on the stride.

Ramps

Ramps are easy to walk on and to push wheelchairs, prams, and wheelbarrows up to another level. If intended for this use, however, they should not be more than a 6 percent gradient. In gardens it is unusual to build ramps; they require so much space that too much of the garden would be taken up. Only on sloping sites which are not overly steep is it feasible to construct a climbing, winding path that looks at ease in the garden while still remaining functional. Combinations of a ramp next to steps are rare in gardens, although a good example can be seen in Vienna's Belvedere Garden. Such combinations require great design skill to be successful.

Stepped ramps

A good compromise are stepped ramps. The ramps should not exceed 6 percent, the steps, a uniform distance apart, make up the difference and shorten the run. Stepped ramps are both easy and effortless to climb, a popular form of step found in old towns and villages around the Mediterranean. Here not only pedestrians but also horses and mules had to use the steps, as this was often the only way of getting from one level to another. Due to the amount of space needed, stepped ramps are seldom found in private gardens. They are seen more often in public parks and then only over short distances.

Block steps and tread slabs require a stable and professionally constructed base. For large stairs, it is essential to lay a concrete form, depending on the size based on structural calculations and with the necessary reinforcement. It is on this base that the steps are bedded in mortar. Even the smallest flight of steps should have the first riser firmly bedded on a concrete base.

Simplified schematic sections for the various types of steps, using the same dimensions in each case for riser and tread.
From top to bottom: Block steps, tread steps, retaining steps, and ramped steps. Depending on the number of steps, the overall length of the flight, and the ground conditions, a concrete foundation may be necessary. Always check the local building regulations when designing and building steps.

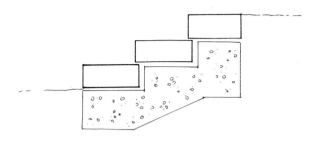

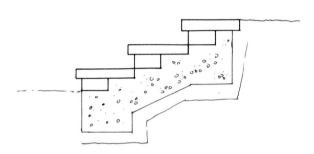

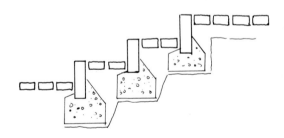

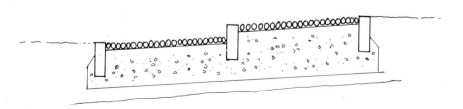

Opposite page: Not all steps are intended for use. In this example the two steps lead to a sunken garden which cannot be entered but only admired from above.

Brick is an excellent building material for all types of steps. As these photographs illustrate, there are many variations:

Right: The upper portion of an exceptionally long flight of steps edged with a low concrete side wall. Instead of a balustrade a thick hedge flanks and frames the steps.

Far right: Garden steps bordering on shrubberies should always be built wider than necessary, as overhanging vegetation reduces the effective width. Any extra space makes an ideal display area for pots.

Below: The semi-circular brick steps seem to grow out of the plinth of the house. Wider steps may need additional handrails.

An interesting detail that can be readily copied is the use of risers as a planting surface. Not only the ivy shown in this example but all low growing, ground hugging plants are suitable.

Above: To facilitate a change in direction for a flight of steps, plan a landing.

Left: Ramped steps, a combination of ramps and steps, are very practical for enabling wheelbarrows and other equipment to reach all levels.

Next page: It is not always desirable for steps to dominate the garden. Steep steps with narrow treads are particularly difficult to design successfully. Here is an exceptionally good example of what is possible.

Criteria for the Selection of Hard Ground Surfaces

Next page: If materials and plants are well coordinated it is possible to create illusions such as this Provencal garden in the middle of London.

Choosing the right paving from the enormous range and tempting examples available is difficult enough for the professional; for the layperson it is a confusing and daunting task. Rules of thumb can make the job easier and help in assessing the suitability of a particular material for your own garden. Although the majority of surface materials are selected according to their appearance, other aspects play an equally important role. Alongside fundamental considerations such as durability and cost are environmental aspects. Simply listing all these criteria can speed up the decision-making process and ensure that the best surface is chosen. The following points are only guidelines, indicating the best route to your "ideal" paving.

Style and Local Character

The primary rule is to use local materials wherever possible. Not only do these blend in better with the surroundings but they have stood the test of time and still look good. The traditional distribution of building materials should not be ignored. "Traditional" need not be synonymous with "old-fashioned;" modern design solutions *are* possible with traditional materials. Many of these are timeless and have their rightful place in virtually every scheme. Looking broadly at the geology of any country there are landscapes dominated by stone as well as areas dominated by clay. Although cheaper transportation has made a

Right: A symphony in natural stone: steps, walls, floor surface, and ornament all come together to produce a very special ambiance.

larger range of products more widely available from other areas, good quality, inexpensive (particularly second-hand) material can still be found locally.

The context also influences the choice. While an indigenous, more rustic natural-style material is at home in the countryside, exotic materials and bold design are more successful in an urban environment. Concrete is a case in point. While this material looks out of place in the countryside, it takes on a different character in an urban setting, appearing more in harmony with the overall picture.

The building style and materials of the house are important points to bear in mind when selecting materials for the adjacent hard surfaces. Contrasts between old and new create interest, but only succeed if designed with care. Picking up the theme of existing

building material and reflecting it in the paths and terraces works much better. Motifs and ornament used in the design of the house can be incorporated in the floorscape, thus creating a direct link between the building and the garden.

The atmosphere of a garden is greatly influenced by the hard surfaces. This is never more so than in winter when the hard surfaces supply color and interest at an otherwise dull time. Paving must be appropriate from the beginning and carried throughout the garden in a uniform style. Basically, hard surfaces can be divided into either formal or natural. Formal paving is characterized by precise edges and a certain degree of finish, and includes slabs, paving stones, bricks, and decking. Natural surfaces on the other hand are comprised of loose material such as gravel, wood chips, "green paving" such as grass, and paving with grass joints, rubble stones, and pebbles.

Function and Performance

Both the use of the surface and the demands which will be placed on it are important and worthy of consideration. Not all materials and formats are suitable for vehicular traffic, for example, even if this is only occasional. Mosaic paving is purely a pedestrian surface. Distortion, hollows, cracks, and displacement will result if surfaces are used by

heavier loads than intended. In gardens, the estimated load bearing requirements are easy to assess. It is not expected that a terrace or garden path will be driven upon, except perhaps by a lawn mower. The classification of load bearing capabilities of hard surfaces ranges from:

• heavy traffic (continual vehicular use)

• medium heavy traffic (cars and occasional transport vehicles)

• light traffic (occasional cars, bicycles and pedestrians)

The traffic classification determines both the road construction and the type of surface bond that can be used. A professionally constructed stable sub-base is essential to support the top visible layer of paving. The sub-base is a permeable base, which also distributes the load evenly and ensures that any movement caused by freezing or thawing is prevented. Uneven surfaces, dislodged stones, or hollows are all signs of a faulty or inadequate base. All hard surfaces in the garden may be considered as surfaces for light traffic, with the exception of the garage entrance, parking spaces, and drives, all of which are areas of medium-heavy traffic.

Old paving incorporated into the garden takes on a new life with partial plant covering and spontaneous growth in the joints.

Size and Shape

The size and shape of the area to be paved also influences the choice of material. Clear geometric shapes demand a different treatment from flowing organic forms. Difficult alignments of terraces and paths take on different appearances when paved with an agreeable material. Optical tricks (easy to achieve with brick paving) distort and seemingly reshape an area. Small areas appear larger if small sized paving is used. The relationship of joint size to the paving unit is of major importance, as is the size of the material to the bond. The secret is to keep a close eye on the proportions.

The Comfort Factor

In public areas, comfortable and pedestrian-friendly surfaces are highly valued.

A criticism often raised against paving stones is their uneven surface and the danger of high heels wedging themselves in joints. The real reason for this is not the paving stones themselves but bad workmanship. Tight, regular joints between quality material make for a good paving stone surface, which is then a joy to walk over. Part of the garden experience is experiencing a variety of surfaces - the contrast between crunching gravel, smooth bricks, and soft bouncy wood chips. Even so, wobbly garden furniture on uneven terraces is as unwanted as protruding corners of tiles and slabs on which to stub one's toes. Well laid surfaces should not be traps!

Vertical and horizontal color. The green of the climbers is echoed in the joints of the paving. This is not just for visual effect, it is also environmentally sound. Rain water can filter through the wide joints thus returning to the water table.

Paving and Permeability

In many cities and districts the use of permeable paving is a requirement, an environmental necessity enforced by municipal legislation. Surface water that is neither dirty nor contaminated must be allowed to rejoin the water table and so help to replenish ever falling levels. Permeable hard surfaces are any that allow surface water to pass through either the materials themselves or the joints. These include all natural paving stones and slabs, bricks and concrete unit paving, and of course gravel. In contrast to the newer slightly porous concrete paving (developed to allow a certain percentage of water to filter through the concrete), other materials allow precipitation only to penetrate via the joints. A high proportion of joints is therefore advanta-

geous. It is also important to ensure that the sub-base consists of coarse grained material, which allows water to filter though and ultimately reach the water table.

Secondhand with Character

Not only new material fresh from the quarry or factory can be purchased, but also used material. In Europe, for example, an active trade in "old paving," including a large variety of materials, shapes, and sizes imported from the former Eastern Block countries, has brought new life to the market. City and local authorities are often good sources for material that is a by-product of the repair and renewal of roads. Rare mosaic stones and old fashioned brick sizes, required for restoration work in conservation areas, can only be obtained through these sources. Often it is only used material that has the necessary patina required to blend into the historical fabric. In historic house gardens, second-hand material radiates the required traditional atmosphere immediately.

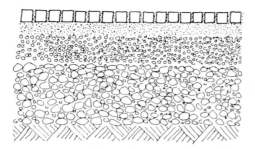

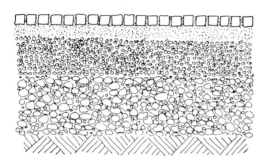

Section through a small element paving stone surface for medium-heavy traffic (courtyards, parking areas etc.):
• Small element paving stones (3/4")
• Bedded in 2" split (stone grit) or sharp sand

• Base, comprising 8-12" compacted gravel
• Frost protection layer, 1'-1'8" gravel compacted in layers, depth according to ground conditions

Section through a small element paving stone surface designed for heavy traffic (roads):
• Small element paving stones (3/4")
• Bedded in 2" split (stone grit)
• Base, minimum 1' depth, of compacted gravel
• Frost protection layer, 1'-1'8" gravel compacted in layers

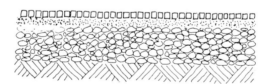

Section through mosaic paving stone surface for light traffic (garden paths and terraces):
• Mosaic paving stone (1-2")
• Bedded in 1 1/2 - 2" split (stone grit) or

sharp sand on level, firm base
• Base/frost protection layer, 8-12" compacted gravel; in areas with well draining subsoil such as gravel this layer is not required

The Limits of "Do-it-Yourself"

The apparent ease with which paving can be laid is misleading. The process of laying paving is graded according to degree of difficulty. Only talented amateurs should attempt to lay very difficult paving and only then with full knowledge of the extent of the task. In general, flagstones, brick, and concrete units are simpler to lay than natural paving stones. Paving stones, in particular small element and mosaic, should be left to the experienced pavior. After extended training, an accomplished pavoir masters the whole spectrum of bonding patterns and is knowledgeable about materials and their use. Gravel surfaces and grass paths create few problems and are within the capabilities of most gardeners. Pebble mosaics on the other hand require artistic talent and patience. Since paving patterns are built upon geometrical principles similar to those of tailors, the lines must be adhered to or the fit will not be attained. If you value your leisure time you must have a clear and honest opinion of your capabilities, acknowledge your limitations, and make your choice accordingly.

Below: A modern design using geometric forms and patterns in a limited mixture of materials.

Right: The design language of the house is reflected in the choice of paving material: a clear and symmetrical stage-like deck with sunken pool forms a continuation of the building.

Paving - A Luxury Item?

Even after all the above points have been carefully studied, every designer will be confronted with the constraints imposed by cost. Far too often, compromises must be made and a cheaper alternative to the first choice selected. A useful method of estimating cost includes not only a consideration of the initial capital cost but also that of subsequent maintenance and the expected lifespan of the material. Working on this basis, a far more realistic figure is obtained. What at first seems inexpensive paving, for example, may last only a few years with no chance of reuse if alterations to the path or terrace are made. New material would be required, involving further cost. Had a better quality material been used from the outset, the second outlay would not have been necessary. Calculated in this way affordability takes on a new perspective. To quote figures with today´s fluctuating prices is of little help. The following list graduating from the least to most expensive includes materials and labor costs and should be used as a rough guide only:

Grass paths
Wood chips
Gravel (from normal rocks, not specials such as Carrara marble)
Hoggin
Concrete slabs
Timber modules

Clay brick paving
Concrete unit paving
Clinker paving
Stone slabs (depending on the stone, the cost varies from affordable to expensive)
Timber decking
Paving Stones (large, small, and mosaic sizes in that order)

Do not forget that price is linked to quality; just as not all concrete is cheap, not all natural stone is expensive. It is a great help to ask the approximate costs per square foot, and estimate the size of the area to be paved before commissioning the job. Edging is often not included in the price and is quoted per running foot. As this quantity can be quite substantial, it should not be forgotten.

Doing the work yourself is not always the most economical alternative. Not only must the material be bought, the necessary equipment and tools must be purchased or rented. If the cost of labor were included in the total figure, it would be considerable. Even so, the desire to try paving on your own can be hard to resist. At the end of the day the result is either permanent proof of one's capabilities or the reminder of an excruciating, laborious task. Often a compromise is best. Large areas can be left to the contractor while smaller simple paving or special ornaments, motifs, and vignettes can be designed and built by the individual. Paving, particularly in brick and natural stone, is a definite investment. It can both improve the appearance and increase the value of a property.

Look and Test

Sample areas, finished schemes, and illustrations in books or magazines are useful aids in decision-making. Small areas, however, give a different impression than larger ones. Single paving samples viewed indoors look different outside in daylight. Do not be afraid of walking over paved areas. Test how comfortable a surface is, how well garden furniture stands on it. Build up your own experience and judge critically whether the building material, house style, paving material, and bonding pattern are suitable. Collect your own reference library of examples. The aim is to select a hard surface that is not only long lasting, but also complements and enhances your garden, is within your budget, and is capable of accommodating changing tastes.

Natural Stone

Next page: As time goes by, natural stone takes on a patina making it a neutral mellow background suitable for any garden. The generous sized natural stone path shown here is both an ideal companion to and barrier between the vibrant flower beds.

Without a doubt, everyone would love to use natural stone paving in the garden; the cost of this material, however, combined with the cost of its placement puts many off. Among the wide selection of hard surface materials, the number of natural stone imitations is amazing. Through their appearance and durability all attempt to be cheaper alternatives to the real thing. Stone has been declared a luxury item, an aristocratic or rustic material, supposedly with a place only in exclusive suburbs or chic shopping malls. Yet a closer look at many streets reveals that natural stone can still be seen, even if only as a modest but functional curb. The attraction of stone lies not only in its variety of shapes, textures, and colors, but also in its ability to fit well into any setting.

Stone paving ranges from unsorted pebbles at the lower end of the scale, to hand worked, carefully selected marble mosiac paving stones at the other. The price of paving material depends on the ease with which it can be quarried, the quantities available, and the quality. For every expensive stone there is generally a similar but cheaper alternative. Once laid, natural stone is there for future generations. Not only does the material retain its value, it can also be reused. Environmentally sound and economically viable, the versatility and adaptability of natural stone is unending. Provided the material has been properly laid, maintenance should be minimal: when regularly used the joints stay free of growth, when walked upon infrequently a

Assorted sizes of large paving stones laid in rows abutting granite flagstones.

green shimmer of grass, moss, or weeds will develop.

Hard paving is often chosen for its appearance, color, and texture. However, thought must be given also to wear and tear, the ability to survive frost and resist pollution, and above all, suitability for the location. "Exotics" may be dynamic and add that extra sparkle but can be out of place or totally unsuitable for the particular climate or conditions.

A Brief Guide to Stone

This survey of the most important and common types of stone concentrates on their color, structure, and suitability for use as paving material. It is intended only as a general guide. If further detailed information is required, consult a geological textbook which covers the formation and distribution of rocks in greater depth. Beware of the differences between geological and commercial names, which can often be confusing when dealing with building materials. Depending on the type of stone, some material is better suited for cutting into slabs and paving stones than others. In all cases, knowledge of the basic stone characteristics is useful. The following points should be considered during the selection procedure:

• The frost tolerance of the stone. Bear in mind that regional climatic differences, particularly the frequency and degree of ground frost, limit the choice of suitable paving material.

• The weathering and wearing characteristics of the stone. Virtually all stones darken with age; this is a natural process caused by exposure and use.

Many mosaic paving stone surfaces completed at the beginning of the century demonstrate the variety of material available. This example shows dark basalt, grey granite, red-brown sandstone, and violet porphyry.

New red-brown sandstone small element paving stones (Kirtschevit from Bulgaria) laid in segmental arcs. Karlshofer Weser hard sandstone or grey-brown Ruhr sandstone are equally suitable paving materials.

New yellow-grey granite small element paving stones laid in segmental arcs. As this particular color of stone is quarried from upper layers, not all yellow granites are one hundred percent frost tolerant.

- The availability and range of sizes.

- The function of the paved area and the load bearing requirements.

Natural stone comes into its own only in the right location and if professionally and correctly laid. Even the most beautiful and expensive stone can fail if wrongly used.

Granite

Granites form one of the largest and most varied groups of all paving materials. The best known and most widespread of igneous rocks, granite is frequently associated only with grey tones yet is much more varied. In addition to the common colors, virtually every shade from dark red, yellow, and even blue and green tones can be found. As a rule, unusual colors belong to the exotic granites. These are only to be had in small quantities at a premium price and are not always suitable for outdoor use.

The appearance of the stone as well as its color is affected by the granular size. Depending on this size, granite is classified as either fine, medium, or coarse grained. Granite is cut into slabs and paving stones of all sizes, is extremely weatherproof, and is an ideal hard surface for use in the garden.

Gneiss

Commercially listed as a rock classification in its own right, the name refers in fact to a pooling of two different rocks that are similar in appearance - orthogneiss and paragneiss. Orthogneiss is an igneous rock, similar to granite in appearance but with a foliated structure and consequently easier to split. Colors range from pink to grey, orange, brown,

and black, in all shades and combinations. Gneiss is primarily available as slabs.

Paragneiss, Beola

Depending on its origin, this sandy, clay sedimentary rock can be either of granite, quartzite, or dioritic composition. It is supplied as slabs or paving stones and is often simply referred to as "split granite" or "quartz." It is also frequently referred to by the name of the quarry where it is found, such as Beola and Magglia, both of which are in Italy. Striped or sprinkled, the colors range from grey-white to blue-green with a slight silvery glint.

Syenite and Diorite

Both are igneous rocks related to granite and are often sold as granite. As they are similar, it can be easy to confuse the two. They can, however, be identified by color: syenite is red, light red, or sometimes grey or pink, while diorite is coarse grained and dark green or black. Neither are readily available now, although second-hand material from the turn of the century is occasionally found.

Porphyry (Rhyolith)

The attraction of porphyry, in fact quartzporphyry (now classified as Rhyolith), lies in its color range from dark red, purple, red-brown, to green. The quality of the rock varies from quarry to quarry. As a rule porphyry from deep layers is frost resistant, that quarried on the surface is not guaranteed to be so. Sheering and fissures are signs of poorer quality material, however both become apparent only after the material has been laid and exposed to wear and tear. It is essential to obtain a certificate of frost and salt resistance from the supplier or quarry. Bear in mind this

must relate to the specific climatic zone where the stone will be used. Porphyry is supplied as slabs, small element and mosaic paving stones, and as ornamental gravel.

Porphyroid

Orthogneiss, which originates from porphyry, is often classified as porphyriod. In this category are the green, so-called *Graubundener* natural stone slabs, which are used a great deal in garden schemes in Europe.

Sandstone

Sandstones are sedimentary rocks. They form a large group of rocks, laid down in different ways, with different geological classifications. They vary in color depending on their substance. Many are hard, durable, and weather well, while others are softer. It is advisable, therefore, to obtain precise information about the hardness of the chosen stone. It is usually safe to assume that those sandstones available through good commercial sources have been tested to meet all requirements. As sandstones are so widespread, virtually every country has a good supply. Not all sandstone is used as paving stones, much more is available as slabs.

Greywacke

As a sedimentary rock, greywacke is used primarily in areas with little or no ground frost. In comparison to other sedimentary rocks it has a high compressive strength. Quarrying and splitting into regular blocks is comparatively easy. Greywacke is made into large, small element, and mosaic paving stones. The color of this fine grained rock ranges from yellowish grey to beige.

Limestone and marble

Limestone is a well-known building material. A few types are also suitable for use in the garden, but can be susceptible to weathering. The colors of limestone available for flagstones and large, small element, and mosaic paving stones vary from dark blue-grey to light white-beige.

Marble, a crystalline limestone, is not only a favorite interior flooring, but can also be used with great ornamental effect in combination with other garden paving. Some types of fine pored marble can even be used in areas with heavy ground frost. Depending on mineral content the colors range from black, grey, red, and green, to white. One of the most famous white marbles, Carrara, is named after the area from which it is quarried in Italy and is widely used in ornamental floorscapes. Other types of marble are white and grey Astir from Greece and white Lasa from southern Tyrol. In addition to slabs, marble is also supplied as small element and mosaic paving stones, ornamental sharp sand, and gravel.

Slate

This is a laminated, light to dark grey rock which can be split along lines of cleavage to produce thin slates. Used widely in the past as a roofing material, slate can also be used in thicker form as paving slabs in the garden. Material comes from Norway and, in Britain, from the traditional slate quarries in Wales and the Lake District.

Quartzite

A crystalline slate, formed by the metamorphosis of former sandstones. Very easily split, it is available as rough quarry slabs and as small element or mosaic paving stones in red, white brown-grey, or grey shades. Quartzite is durable and forms a good surface to walk on.

Basalt

Basalt forms the largest group of igneous rocks. Dense and fine grained, it is a smooth, dark-grey, nearly black rock. When exposed to strong sun, basalt can become patchy and split. For this reason it is generally only available in small sizes. At the turn of the century, basalt paving stones were commonly used as street and ornamental paving. The surface is very slippery when wet, however, and basalt fell out of favor as a result. After many years of rejection, basalt is experiencing a comeback as an ornamental material in private and municipal schemes and can be purchased as newly quarried paving stones.

Diabase (Dolerite)

Diabase forms a group within the magma rocks, all of which have similar characteristics. It is a basalt that through aging (chemical erosion) has turned green. It is known under a variety of names, including "Greenstone." The grain size varies from fine to coarse and the rocks have a high compressive strength. Colors range from grey-green to dark blue green. Diabase is produced as slabs, paving stones, and as a dark green ornamental gravel.

Trachyte

Trachyte is an igneous, often porous stone of light colors such as yellow, brown to red, and more rarely pure white. Much of this stone comes from Italian quarries; it is supplied as paving stones and slabs but is not widely available. The name trachyte (derived from the Greek word for roughness), indicates the nature of the slightly rough surface. Trachyte is often confused with porphyry.

**Anthracite colored
slate flagstones after
a shower of rain.**

Does the grass grow out of the path or the path out of the grass? A seamless transition with the added bonus of strong color contrast.

Below: Second-hand "Charlottenburger Slabs" in 12, 16, and 20" widths, dressed from larger broken slabs, sawn and hand finished.

Stone Slabs: Shapes and Bonds

Paths and terraces paved in natural stone can be magnificent. Stone is versatile and suited to virtually any setting, from old world rustic to classic elegance and even ultra modern. Technical advancements in quarrying and stone cutting have enabled quantity production. The face, or the top visible surface of the slab, can be treated in a number of ways. Depending on the finishing process a variety of surface textures can be achieved. The more work required the more expensive the finished product. The following brief explanation of technical terms describes the appearance of the various finishes.

Naturally split slabs, known as rubble, uncut, or quarry-pitched stone, are characterized by irregular shapes and sizes and raw unworked surfaces. Uneven surfaces full of character are part of the attraction for this cheap material, which can often be laid directly on the ground. Because of their rough, indented surface, the slabs are unsuitable for terraces (especially if garden furniture is to be placed on them), but do suit paths and fringe areas in country or natural gardens quite well.

Broadly speaking, **sawn slabs** are divided between single faced slabs and those sawn on two faces. Depending on the stone type and load bearing qualities, they are available in various thicknesses. Uniform sized slabs and those of random length are cut from two faced sawn slabs. Ashlar regular sized slabs are rectangular or square, have fixed sizes, and

are generally more expensive than those with random lengths, which are characterized by constant width and thickness, but are delivered in varying lengths. How the edges of the slabs are finished, whether uncut or quarry pitched stone (irregular), sawn (regular), or hand-dressed (precise and sharp) is important. Outdoor paving must provide good grip and be slip-proof. Highly polished stones are not only dangerous when wet, they can look out of place in gardens.

Quarry pitched slabs are worked to approximate sizes. The surface is dressed with a hammer, giving more textural depth, and is nearly quarry rough in appearance. It is one of the least expensive finishes. **Tooled slabs**, in which the surface (face) is chiseled using a pointed tool, takes on a different appearance depending on the degree to which it is worked. A tooled surface retains grip, yet is not uncomfortable to walk over.

Coarsely tooled slabs look similar to rough quarry stones, but are not as uneven as a hammered finish. Fine and medium-fine slabs have a lively surface with obvious traces of workmanship.

Pick finished, or picked, slabs are also graded according to the degree to which they are worked - either fine, medium, or coarse. The surface is slightly rough and the structure and veins are visible. This finish is particularly suitable for terraces or areas adjoining the house.

Sandblasted slabs have a particularly fine grained, only slightly roughened surface. The overall effect is flat and matte.

Furrows or grooves are a detail carried out on prepared surfaces and used generally as decoration. They are ideal as a slip-proof finish for treads. As a rule, a 1 inch to 3 inch wide band immediately behind the riser is carefully and evenly worked with a special tool using short strokes at right angles to the leading edge of the tread.

New slabs, fresh from the quarry, darken when exposed to the elements and when used. Virtually no stone, with the exception of marble, keeps its original showroom appearance. This is not necessarily a drawback, as the stone acquires its own specific color. **Flamed slabs**, which have been thermally treated, are new, "old stones," as they have a similar texture and color to naturally weathered rocks.

The choice of bond depends on the size and shape of the slabs. Rough quarry stones can only be laid in a **random bond**, with irregular joints and staggered edges; this is commonly known as "crazy paving." Due to the nature of these slabs, paths made from them tend to have slightly varying widths without clean cut edges to adjoining areas. Similar to this bond, but laid with slabs that have been roughly hewn to size, is **Cyclopean paving**. Here, large irregular shaped slabs are laid adjacent to each other with narrow joints. The Greeks and Romans were masters of this paving. Many examples can still be found in Italy, Spain, and Greece.

Rectangular and square slabs (ashlar) can be laid in a variety of ways. Traditionally, these slabs are laid with staggered joints in **stretcher bond.** A variation of this is **running bond**. Here the slab width is constant but the lengths vary. Any number of variations are possible, depending on the rhythm of the lengths and the number of slabs. When very long and narrow slabs are used, the method is referred to as a **"planking bond."**

The overall effect of paving is determined not only by the slabs but also the joints. These wide mossy joints between the polygonal stone slabs accentuate the semi-shade planting.

Below: Stepping stones in the lawn indicate which route to take while at the same time protecting the lawn.

For a more formal effect, identically sized and finely finished slabs can be laid in **stack bond,** which is also known as cross bond or jack on jack. The crossed, unbroken joints of this surface give it limited load bearing capacity and it is suitable only for pedestrian use. In virtually all other bonds besides stack bond the joints are staggered, thus avoiding lateral movement and displacement if used by heavier loads.

Other important bond considerations are that the width of the joint must be in proportion to the slab size, and that all surfaces must be laid with a minimum 2 percent cross fall away from the building.

To achieve a lively, interesting bond, uniform slab sizes can be mixed with others. Ultimately the choice of bond is governed by personal taste. If unsure of the overall effect, however, it is preferable to stick to one bond. Only experienced paviors can develop their own combinations based on the basic bonds.

Stepping stones

In gardens, it is not always necessary for all paths to be fully paved. Stepping stones on lawns, through plant beds, or even across unusual paving material that is not particularly comfortable to walk on, can look quite pleasing. The design possibilities are infinite. When setting out the stones a stride length of 2 feet 2 inches enables most people to walk from stone to stone without hopping. Ensure that the slabs are large enough to stand on with both feet and that they are all of roughly similar size.

Combinations of different materials are possible in a garden setting. Gravel not only frames and emphasizes the rectangular and square stepping stones, it also widens the path.

This stone paved path demonstrates the variety of large stone sizes. Within an individual delivery the stones may also have differing thicknesses, which makes correct laying difficult.

The Renaissance of Paving Stones

What was once a common street paving material at the end of the nineteenth century in Europe and North America is now a part of history. With its demise, the craft and skill of the master pavior has become virtually lost. Recent awareness of the environment, together with increasing interest in the potential of natural materials and promotion of the use of local materials, has caused a reappraisal of hard surface material. Combined with the specific goal of creating more durable streetscapes, this reappraisal has prompted great interest in paving stones. Private gardens as well as civic ones can benefit from the use of this high quality material.

In Germany, Austria, France, Northern Italy, and Portugal the art of paving stone production and laying is still nurtured. Master paviors are highly qualified craftsmen, trained to high standards until they have mastered the material and its use. The absence of any official English language specifications that can be used by designers and contractors alike makes the control of good working practice in other areas difficult. Standards used in Germany provide an insight into working practice and standards which should be the goal for all work using paving stones. These standards apply only to new paving stones (large, small element, and mosaic) quarried within Germany, specifically granite, basalt, diorite, greywacke, and melaphyr. Although paving stones from other countries are not bound by these standards, they are generally sorted according to size and subjected to quality control. Nonetheless, variations in size and color in a delivery can occur. Additionally, poor material has sometimes been passed off among good. For this reason, it is essential to purchase material from a recognized quality supplier or direct from the quarry. Scotland has taken a lead in promoting quality control in the supply of paving stones and has even developed a "paving stone bank" of local material for the benefit of civic projects. The lack of recognized quality control in many other countries means the purchaser must specify exactly what is required when ordering paving stones.

As with all quarried stone, a distinction is made between the top (face) and the bottom of a stone. Every paving stone has an obvious face, which as a rule is smoother and slightly larger than the bottom. The top should always be laid on the surface. Badly executed paving is characterized by the top and bottom having been confused, thereby producing a very irregular, pitted, and uncomfortable surface.

Right: Among the many special sizes of second-hand large paving stones are the distinctive "Viennese Cubes." When laid in rows binder-stones or one-and-a halves are necessary. A characteristic feature of used paving stones is the smooth surface as visible on the paving stones to the far right.

Unusual paving stone shapes come to life in the garden. As a rule they are available only in small quantities, so use them as features.

Below: A decorative surface covered with bishop´s mitres and cubes.

Below right: "Horse paving stones," a large paving stone (5 1/2 - 7") with a deep groove in the middle. The groove looks like a joint and draws attention to the length. This stone is rare and only occasionally available on the second-hand market.

The degree of
workmanship is
clearly visible in this
example. The sawn
and hand dressed
small element and
large new paving
stones are charac-
terized by sharp
edges and regular
sizes.

Mosaic paving
stones can be laid in
all manner of bonds.
Here, for example,
they are laid in rings
to form a semicircle
signaling the top of
a flight of steps. The
rest of the area is in
segmental arcs.

Standard Paving Stone Sizes

Large Paving Stones

Large paving stones have acceptable
widths of 6 - 7 inches, lengths from 6 1/2 - 8 1/
2 inches, and heights of 5 1/2 - 6 1/2 inches.
Large paving stones of basalt, diorite,
greywacke, and melaphyr are a little smaller,
with widths of 4 1/2 - 6 inches, lengths of 5 1/2
- 8 1/2 inches, and heights of 5 - 6 inches. The
special formats essential for the laying of
many bonds, such as bishop´s mitre and
binders, are worth mentioning. Large paving
stones are used primarily for frequently used
surfaces and those that must withstand heavy
loads.

Small Element Paving Stones

Small element paving stones generally are
split into three groups: those that are 4 x 4 x 4
inches, those that are 3 1/2 x 3 1/2 x 3 1/2
inches, and those that are 3 x 3 x 3 inches.
Specials like triangles and bishop´s mitre (also
known as five cornered stones) can be
supplied but are expensive and rarely ordered.
Small element paving stones can be widely
used, even for vehicular traffic.

Mosaic Paving Stones

The name for this size paving stone is
derived from ancient mosaic paving. Similar to
the small element stones, mosaic paving
stones are divided into three general sizes: 2
1/2 x 2 1/2 x 2 1/2 inches; 2 x 2 x 2 inches;
and 1 1/2 x 1 1/2 x 1 1/2 inches. New material
is available only in the smallest size. Today it is
hard to believe that at the turn of the century
mosaic paving stones were considered a
cheap surface material, although this does
explains why they were so widespread in both
private and municipal schemes. Mosaic paving
stones are only suitable for areas with little or
no vehicular traffic. They are one of the most
important paving stones in gardens.

Fieldstones and Pebbles

In addition to the cut and graded paving stones, some stones are used in their original form. Simply collected in the open countryside or from river beds or banks, such material is primarily used for paving in historic contexts. This does not preclude its use from contemporary schemes or private gardens.

Cobblestones

Cobblestones are 16-10 inch diameter stones, rounded or oval in form, which are laid into the ground or a sandbed without being additionally worked in any way. Many roads were cobbled well into the nineteenth century, producing an uneven, bumpy surface that was uncomfortable to travel over. Graded, hand-picked cobblestones can still be purchased and do look good in gardens, particularly in fringe areas.

A centuries old randomly paved street is successfully integrated into the garden.

Pebbles

These are similar to cobblestones but smaller in size (from pea-size to 5 inches in diameter). Pebbles are smooth, elongated, or egg-shaped. These stones are generally placed lengthwise in the bed or upended with only the top showing. They occur in a variety of sizes and colors, from white, grey and even black, to reds and greens (depending on the rock from which they originate). Their high ornamental potential makes them very popular in gardens.

Split-stones and "Wacke" Stones

Larger pebbles that are split in half are referred to as split-stones. The flat smooth face is exposed as the surface, with the rest of the stone bedded in the ground. The larger the face, the greater depth the stone generally has. A "wacke" stone is split from a solid stone that is substantially larger than a pebble. A forerunner of large paving stones, it can still be found in many old European towns. An interesting new product is "antique wacke" stones. The surface is of the stone is aged with a special process, making it ideal for sensitive areas where freshly split stones would not harmonize with the surroundings.

Cobblestone paving does not offer a level surface but it creates a wonderful atmosphere.

Below: Orderly rows
of granite small
element paving
stone laid with a
level edging, which
flow around the
plant beds.

Right: Net bond
using large granite
paving stones. In
order to lay this
bond, bishop´s
mitres or triangular
paving stones are
essential along the
base line.

The Craft of the Master Pavior

The manner in which the stones are set next to each other is all important. If laid by a master craftsman the paving comes alive. In the hands of an amateur an inharmonious patchwork can result. Through years of experience and highly developed sensitivity a master pavior selects exactly the right stone for each situation. The apparent ease with which the pavior works is deceptive. Every bond is built on certain principles, which can be clearly read. "Let´s give it a try and see what happens" is no maxim for laying paving stones; planning is essential. Part of the preparatory work consists of calculating the amount of material required, constructing the sub-base and bedding, and careful setting out.

In addition to the actual look of a bonding pattern, the following points should be kept in mind when deciding which bond to use:

• Use the correct bond for the stone size. The paving stone size determines the scale of the bonding pattern. Not every paving stone format is suitable for every bonding pattern.

• Choose the right bond for the situation. In other words, one that is appropriate for the size, shape, use, and expected loads.

• Demand good professional working practice; many bonds cannot be laid by amateurs.

The variety of paving patterns, particularly those using dressed stone, originate from the late nineteenth century. This period can be an inspiration to us all.

Ordered chaos

Random Paving

The ultimate form of this paving uses not only different sizes but also different types of material. In this way rubble stones, quarry stones, and primitively split stones can all be used. The result is a lively paving, with a totally irregular network of joints and a melange of colors. Random paving can be one of the hardest patterns to execute as it does not follow any prescribed order and is truly freestyle. The secret lies in chance and spontaneity.

Cobbled Paving

Paving using naturally occurring small round boulders or large pebbles simply rammed into the earth was one of the earliest forms. "Cobbled" is a general term relating more to the material than to one particular bond. It can in fact cover all types of bonds, but is commonly associated with a random bond.

All in a Row

All of the following bonds, which are variations of the stretcher bond, can be laid in large, small element, and mosaic paving stones. It is important to note that areas paved with small formats are not as stable and strong as when laid with large paving stones, which are capable of withstanding the heaviest traffic.

Stretcher Bond

Classic stretcher bond belongs to one of the oldest paving types. The stones are laid beside each other in courses (rows), each course staggered so that no cross joints occur. The starter stone in alternate courses can be a half stone, or for surfaces intended for heavier traffic a binder or one-and-a-half paving stone. This bond is suitable for garden paths and terraces.

Diagonal Bond

Diagonal bond paving is similar to stretcher bond, only with the courses at a 45 degree angle to the direction of the path or terrace. Triangular or five-corner-paving stones (bishop´s mitre) are used at the start of each course, providing a clean edge to the curb and automatically pointing the following paving stones in the right direction. An extended herringbone pattern used in street paving is little more than a refined diagonal bond: two diagonals meet at 90 degrees at the high point in the center of the area or street, the link being formed by a binder stone. Commonly laid in large granite, sandstone, or diorite paving stone, diagonal bond forms a very stable, strong, and durable surface.

Net Paving

In order to achieve a net pattern, square paving stones must be selected and then laid in diagonal rows. The first stone in a row is a triangular special: cross joints are intentional and are an essential part of the bond. Net paving can be produced using any stone size, and has a decorative quality more suitable for gardens than streets. Terraces, paths, and sitting areas can all be paved in this pattern. Marvelous examples of intricate net paving can be seen in Portugal in squares and public parks.

"Passee" Paving or "Broken Ice" Bond

Even though "passee" is not an obvious type of stretcher bond, it definitely cannot be grouped with random or arc paving. The essential character in this type is the change in direction of the joints. On closer examina-tion of what seems at first chaos a system does become apparent. The only rules are that after every fourth or fifth stone the direction should change and that every stone must link into the pattern. The attraction of this bond lies in its "regular" irregularity. The pattern turns and swirls in all directions. In some ways it can be likened to the Chinese "broken ice" pattern which has a shattered surface effect.

The rediscovery of this type of paving highlights its potential use as an ornamental paving for large and small areas. But beware, for not every pavior can lay this pattern. The more complicated ornamental variety, in which one pattern overlays another, is especially difficult and demands great skill. Paved largely with mosaic paving stones or occasionally small element paving stones, this bond is suitable only for pedestrian use but lends itself nicely to areas of all shapes and sizes.

Passee bond in detail. The interpretation varies according to the individual craftsman. Despite the interlocking pattern the surface has limited loadbearing capabilities and is therefore suitable only for pedestrian traffic or the occasional car.

Wall to wall passee bond, a quieter version than that featured on the opposite page and **often found in Portugal. A beautiful paving for small and large areas alike.**

Arc Bonds

The term "arc paving" can be confusing, as an "arc" bond - contrary to popular opinion - does not actually exist. It is rather the collective name for a paving type, based on the circle as a setting out element and including segmental arc bond and fan bond. When pricing work it is essential to differentiate between the two and clearly specify which is meant. Both have different properties and characteristics, fan bond being the more difficult and expensive.

Segmental Arc Bond

Segmental arc bond is one of the most common street and piazza paving patterns in Germany and Northern Italy. It is very versatile and equally well suited to the more intimate scale of private gardens. The setting out of this bond is a based on a circle, in particular a 90 degree segmental arc. The width and height of the arc is calculated according to the size of paving stone used and the width of the path, road, or piazza. This is worked out for each location by the designer or pavior. A fundamental aspect of this bond is that it ends and starts with a half segment and that the arcs point towards the high point. It is usually laid in small element paving stones and is, if correctly carried out on a suitable base and bedded in a split or crushed rock, a durable and strong surface. The interlocking paving stones, held together by joints rammed with granular

Right: Ornament can be generated by function, as demonstrated by this "plait" formed at a low point, where segmental arcs from opposite directions meet.

In order to lay segmental arcs a whole range of sizes within stated tolerances for the category must be supplied. Junctions with channels or edging must always be with a half arc.

Above right: A motif originally designed at the beginning of the century by master pavior Friedrich Wilhelm Noll, reinterpreted as paving for a patio. In this setting the design uses mosaic paving stones and fully paved corners. The arcs are directed towards the high point in the center, and for greater contrast can be laid in different colored paving stones.

Below right: A classic piazza design in segmental arcs, equally suitable for a terrace or (as shown here) for a road junction. The central point is laid as a circle, the diagonals are horseshoe shaped, between which the arcs are paved. Here the ornamental effect is also heightened by introducing colored rows of paving stones.

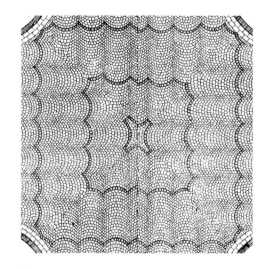

The segmental arc is the most frequently used bond for roads and piazzas and forms a stable loadbearing surface, but this bond works just as well in gardens. Here it is used at the entrance to a house, laid in porhryry small element paving stone. The characteristic wave-like appearance of the surface is always at right angles to the edge of the path or terrace.

material, can withstand heavy loads; if paved with good quality material by professionals, they also provide a comfortable surface to walk on. Mosaic paving stones work well, despite their restricted load bearing properties, but large paving stones are totally unsuitable, being neither appropriate in size or shape for the bond.

Fan Bond or "Fish Scale" Bond

As the name implies, this bond is comprised of repeating fans or fish scales; even without being highlighted by different colored stones these are very decorative. This bond is an ornamental paving suited to terraces and piazzas, and can be used in combination with other paving types. The construction is based on semicircles, all with the same radius. The fan shape is achieved by centering a semicircle directly above two adjacent semicircles. The fan is then filled out with arched rows.

As with segmental arc bond, the radius used depends on the width of the terrace, path, or piazza and, most importantly, the size of paving stone used. Both small element and mosaic paving stones can be used. Large paving stones are far too cumbersome and do not suit the delicate pattern. The general rule is: the larger the paving stone, the greater the radius. Fan bond demands skill and much preparatory work. Both the number of fans and their direction must be determined. The starting point of the bond, whether from the center or the base line, must be decided. The geometry of the bond must be adhered to strictly. This means finishing at the edges with a half fan and starting from the base line with a semicircle or from the midpoint with a full circle. The division and setting out of the area must be completed before the paving stone laying begins.

By using different colored paving stones, the ornamental quality of the area can be emphasized, as in the "Lily" or "Florentina" pattern, in which the outer rows of the fans are picked out.

Half-fans

Half-fans are popular as borders and ornamental friezes on piazzas, terraces, and wide paths. The fans are split lengthwise, to produce a repeating mirror image pattern. As with full fans, the radius must be carefully calculated and should be in proportion to the size of the total area. Changes in direction, such as when framing a rectangular piazza, are achieved using full circles at the corners. To emphasize the half-fans, one or more rows of the same sized, but different colored paving stones should be laid around the frieze. Examples would be a basalt or marble frame laid around granite, or greywacke laid around phorphyry.

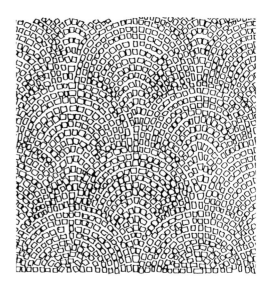

Fans generated from semicircles placed along side each other are impressive even without additional ornament. The variations rendered possible through the use of different colored stones to highlight the construction are innumerable.

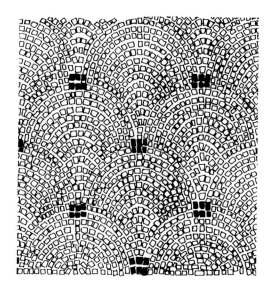

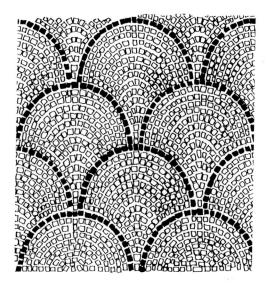

The base of the fans is emphasized and the resulting pattern seems to overlay that of the fans.

A strong graphic effect is created by picking out the central section and long tail of the fan.

In the so-called "Lily" pattern the outer row or rows of the fan are highlighted in a different colored stone.

Rings of different stone types and paving stone sizes set in porphyry paving are more suitable for a large piazza-like terrace. Reduced and laid in mosaic paving stones this pattern can also be used in smaller areas.

Circle Bond

As expected, in this bond full circles are paved. The starting point is the center of the circle, which can be highlighted by using colored paving stones. The concentric rings are laid using smaller material towards the center and larger on the outside. Attention must be paid to the joint size, and for this reason small element and mosaic paving stones are better suited than large paving stones. The paved circles work better as individual motifs rather than as the total covering for an area.

Next page: The ornamental fan motif is a highlight of the pavior´s art. In this example the base of the fan is formed by a block of four carrara marble paving stones, the outline by grey paving stones, and the filling with yellow granite paving stones.

Concrete - Contemporary Material or Cheap Alternative?

Praised by some yet scorned by others, concrete paving still suffers from its image as a cheap substitute. Indeed, if we consider the selection of concrete slabs and unit paving available it is hard to believe that buried beneath all this mediocrity is a material that can be of the highest quality as well as aesthetically pleasing. Used correctly, concrete can be the material of today and, in its most elegant forms, a complement to modern architecture. Even when used in conjunction with natural stone or brick, concrete can look attractive. A narrow strip of simple concrete slabs laid between flower beds becomes an unassuming and modest foil to the plant life. This is in total contrast to the harsh brutal way in which concrete is too often used in public footpaths and civic areas.

Treat every type of rustic or antique concrete imitation with great caution. Beware of marquetry designs using interlocking concrete units, especially colored zigzag wave patterns. They are not only dated but also in bad taste (unless you are intentionally seeking a "kitsch" effect).

Concrete is a material worth serious study. One distinct advantage is its sheer range and versatility, which is continually being developed and extended. It offers not only a wide range of surface textures but a broad palette of colors, ranging from subtle tones to brash primaries. When selecting which concrete to use consider both the functional requirements of the elements and the character of the house style you wish to create.

Roughened alpine-grey concrete block paving contrasts with smooth light brown blocks. The variety of colors, finishes, and shapes of concrete paving is vast.

Concrete Paving Slabs

These have been used for decades and are among the most popular and common hard surfaces used in the garden. They are readily available in a range of square and rectangular shapes from 2 inches to 4 inches thick, in a extensive palette of colors, sizes, and textures. The thicker 3 inch to 4 inch slabs can even withstand heavy loads providing they are laid on the correct base. By using a variety of additives the makers offer a wide spectrum of finishes, ranging from smooth to rough, light to dark, and "futuristic" to "natural."

In some areas, the traditional grey footpath slab has been given a new lease of life in the garden. It is an inexpensive material, compatible with any situation, and versatile in use. It can be used in blocks of four as stepping stones laid in gravel, in conjunction with brick paving, or on its own over larger areas; the design variations are infinite.

Stone Faced Concrete

This is a new and promising development. Thin slabs of natural stone are given a reinforced concrete backing to which they are carefully keyed using oblique channels and a special mortar. The choice of overall thickness depends on the particular engineering requirements. The range of sizes available are limited to popular formats such as 19 1/2 inches x 12 inches and 19 1/2 inches x 23 1/2 inches. The base construction and laying are the same as for other kinds of paving slabs. The material is more expensive than the average concrete slab but less than the middle price range for

natural stone. Marketed in Germany under the trade name "Topstone," this is a product to be on the watch for.

Concrete Unit Paving

Concrete as a paving material is best viewed not as a substitute for natural stone paving stones, but as a well designed system of bonding patterns using small units with even surfaces and clean edges. These patterns are marketed under a variety of trade names but are often collectively called "Designer Paving Stones." A particularly good product is the square (8 inches x 8 inches) "Piazza" concrete unit paving, available with five matching corner stones to create an excellent diagonal bond. A good typical system provides a basic variety of units

Precise, light, and modern this terrace is paved in square concrete slabs in stack bond.

(square to rectangular) to make up a standard bond, thus avoiding the need to cut units on site and to give accuracy and speed of laying.

Environmentally Friendly Concrete

There is a growing movement against the large impervious areas of solid concrete often used for parking lots, which effectively prevent rainfall from returning to the water table. In response, several new concrete unit paving products have been developed. These are made of porous concrete with coarse surface finishes, which allows surface water to drain away naturally rather like a sieve. Some even work like a filter, separating traces of oil and gasoline from the rain water and allowing the cleaned water to return to the ground. However, the large pores can clog and for this reason it is not advisable to use this paving in the immediate vicinity of children's sandboxes or adjacent to hoggin paths. Detailed information about these products can be obtained from the manufacturers.

Opposite page:
From the
"Calco-Vario-Line,"™
mother-of-pearl
colored concrete
paving is supplied in
varying widths. It
makes an elegant
paving suitable for a
garden setting.

Long narrow
concrete precast
slabs set in coarse
gravel, a combina-
tion applicable to
many situations.

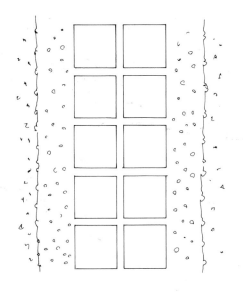

When a path does not need to be fully paved a double row of slabs supplemented by gravel on either side is a good alternative.

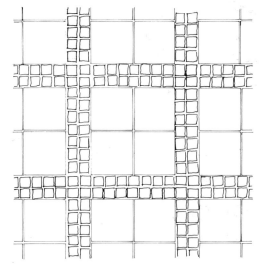

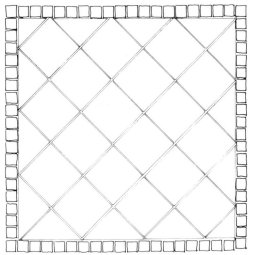

The design possibilities of square concrete paving slabs supplemented by other materials such as granite paving stones are infinite. In this example squares of four slabs are surrounded by two rows of paving stones. This can be repeated as often as is required and forms a good surface for paths and terraces.

Above: A simple pattern like this diagonally laid paving framed by a single row of paving stones is ideal for a square area.

Often seen and often used: common exposed aggregate concrete slabs accompanied by unintended green.

Slick, functional, and complementing the architecture: small concrete blocks laid in stretcher bond.

Below: The accompanying row of irises enhances the significance of this concrete path. The length is further stretched by the orientation of the rectangular slabs.

Next page: This small garden courtyard takes on a new dimension through the gener- ous basket weave brick paving. Path and patio melt into each other.

Clay Brick, Clinker, and Terracotta Paving

It is not without good reason that countless examples of brick paving are illustrated in garden books; few other materials are so useful in the garden. In a well designed garden one´s attention is first drawn by the ambiance and use of plant material; only on closer inspection does the role of the paving become apparent. One recognizes the care which has been given to the choice of color and bond in order to achieve the desired effect. The advantages of brick paving have been known for centuries. Good for walking, with endless design possibilities either alone or in combination with other paving materials, brick is a popular classic.

Below: The manufacturer is immortalized - the initials H & D stand for Heinrich Drasche, a Viennese brick baron from the turn of the century.

These paving bricks are no longer in their original setting but have become a piece of history in a new garden.

A garden path laid in rectangular clinker paving in stretcher bond.

Historically, fired clay was used to produce man-made paving material in areas where natural stone was not readily available. The Romans used mass produced bricks to surface their roads, some of which can still be seen today. The use of brick is no longer restricted to the areas where it is produced. Although some regions still retain a distinct paving culture, improvements in transportation and widening of markets have made the use of brick universal. The choice of material, however, must still be appropriate to its surroundings as well as suited to the area's design and function.

Brick paving lends itself to producing level surfaces, comfortable to walk on and ideal for garden furniture. Brick holds its color; the warm red-brown tones remain as good as the day they were laid even after decades of use. For many projects, especially older buildings or country houses, second-hand material is more fitting than new. Not only can the correct format be used, but the quality and appearance of the paving is a better match.

Clay Brick Paving

Bricks used for building are not necessarily suitable for ground use. A frequent mistake is to ignore the different conditions the bricks are exposed to and then be surprised when cracks appear and the surface crumbles.

Of the three types of bricks,
- commons (wire-cut brick)
- facing (sand mold brick)
- engineering bricks (clinker)

only hard facings and clinker can be recommended for garden use, although well-fired commons can be used in mild climates. In comparison to clinker or engineering bricks, clay bricks are fired at lower temperatures and are consequently less hard and not as long-wearing. They absorb more water, are less able to deal with loads, react with acid, and have limited load-bearing qualities. To tell the difference between brick and clinker, you need only look at the color and do the "ring" test.

Brick is lighter in color, clinker is a more solid, deeper color. When struck, clinker produces a clear "ringing" tone, whereas brick has a noticeably dull, muted tone.

In general, clay bricks are used in Northern Germany, the Netherlands, Belgium, Denmark, England and many parts of North America where milder climatic conditions prevail. Formats and colors vary regionally, even though the standardization of clay brick paving has eliminated many of the differences.

An approximately 2' wide garden path formed by three rows of square clinker pavers is wide enough to walk on comfortably yet does not detract from the flower bed.

Clinker and Engineering Brick Pavers

Clinker paving is a quality product, equally at home in a rustic old world or modern setting. The image of a dull matte product relegated to railway tunnels has become clearly outmoded. While known as clinker in the United States and Europe, in Britain these pavers are referred to as engineering brick. To maintain standards, the quality of clinker paving is constantly tested for its frost and acid tolerance, strength, and other qualities. Clinker made from iron rich clay is fired to fusion point. The temperature is so high that the fragments fuse, the pores disappear, and a very dense pore-free material impervious to water is produced. Clinker is recommended for use outdoors in climates with heavy ground frost and frequent freeze-thaw cycles, as both its durability and frost tolerance are guaranteed. The color is determined by the mineral content in the clay, which varies from pit to pit and can be changed by additives; the scope of colors is therefore no longer limited to the dark dull reds and purple-blues. Ranging from yellow through all the reds to dark brown, the nuances of color are quite fine and can vary within a firing, forming an essential part of the overall aesthetic quality of the material.

Clinker Formats

The dimensions of clinker pavers, both square and rectangular, are based on a grid size ranging from 4 inches to 12 inches. The

minimum thickness is 1 1/2 inches. Dimensions within the grid depend on the manufacturer. As the sizes do vary it is worth checking what is available before starting to order. The following sizes, which can be used as a guide, are based on material supplied in Germany. For detailed local information contact the local, state or federal Brick Association.

Rectangular forms. A list of all available dimensions would be highly confusing. The most common sizes are:

10 inches x 5 inches x 2 1/2 inches
9 inches x 4 1/2 inches x 3 inches
9 inches x 4 inches x 2 inches
8 inches x 4 inches x 2 inches

The surface of the clinker can be textured. The edges can be rounded or sharply defined. Every format is supplied as a full or half paver. Special sizes such as small squares (half bats) and bishop's mitre, vital for several of the more complicated bonds, are available.

Below: These thin Dutch clinker pavers laid in stretcher bond have a strong directional character.

Right: An excellent idea that is rarely seen. Broad brick paved strips create stepping stones across the flower bed to the lawn beyond.

Below: To avoid the appearance of the path being too long and drawn out choose a bond which creates pattern units that can be repeated. This visually divides the path into smaller sections.

Below right: The use of more than one bond can enrich a surface. Here basket weave, divided by a central strip of stretcher bond, has been used for a wide garden path.

Square sizes. The square clinker pavers are generally available in the following sizes:

12 inches x 12 inches
9 1/2 inches x 9 1/2 inches
8 inches x 8 inches
7 inches x 7 inches

Thickness varies from approximately 1 1/2 inches to 3 inches. Although many of these pavers have smooth surfaces, some have a patterned face.

Dutch Clinker Pavers

Dutch bricks are known the world over. Among the various formats, many can now be found only in old paving. These bricks are narrower than those from Germany, being generally only 3 1/2 inches compared with 4 inches or more.

Old Clay Brick Paving

In the past, clay bricks were pressed into their molds by hand. The edges were not as precise as the present machine-produced bricks and the shape varied. Prior to standardization, bricks were produced in small local works. This led to typically local bricks, such as the long narrow clay bricks that typify gardens laid out by the British architect Edwin Lutyens (see page 87). When using old material, check that it is clean and free from cracks.

Opposite page:
Several bonds, such as herringbone and basket weave, are suitable for areas of any size. Here a path widens into a patio. The detailing is worth a closer look. Note the neutral border between the edging and the main surface, as well as the upright edging itself.

Right: Next to the broad limestone edging the bricks appear by contrast to be even more colorful and delicate. Even after the path has been brushed clean the yellow laburnum blossom collects in the joints, emphasizing the herringbone pattern.

Bonds: a Multitude of Variations

An enormous variety of bonds can be laid in brick. The size of the surface, its function, the expected load, and the brick format all play a role in selecting the type of bond. The appropriate brick thickness to be used depends on the load. Footpaths, garden paths, patios, and other areas in the garden should be paved with units that are 1 1/2 - 2 inches thick. Any less and the durability and stability of the surface will be at risk. A higher volume of traffic generally requires thicker bricks. In addition, heavy loads limit the choice of bonds to those in which the stress is passed evenly from unit to unit. Suitable bonds are herringbone and stretcher bond. In gardens where loading is not so great virtually any bond, in any combination, can be used (as long as the overall design intent is still maintained).

As with all paving, a correct sub-base appropriate for the expected load and ground condition is essential. Brick pavers can be laid flat or on edge. Combinations of both can be achieved by laying in a sand bed with a maximum depth of 2 inches. The surface should form one plane and be laid with a fall. Rigid paving, laid in mortar with mortar jointing and sometimes on a concrete foundation, should only be employed in special cases; these would include covered areas, sloping surfaces with a gradient of more than 10 degrees, and industrial sites with a high level of contamination where the surface water may not be fed into the normal drainage.

As colors do tend to differ from pallet to pallet it is sensible to work from several pallets to allow for a good mix.

Stretcher or Running bond. This is one of the simplest, commonest, and easiest of all the bonds. Half bricks are supplied to avoid having to cut bricks on site and to enable the bond to be laid in a professional manner. As when building a wall, the bricks are laid with their face to the surface. The courses are staggered using 1/2, 1/4, or 3/4 brick to prevent cross joints from occurring. This bond is equally suitable for square bricks. A strong directional quality can be achieved if the courses run parallel to the edge of the path. Courses at right angles have the optical effect of widening while simultaneously shortening the apparent length of a path.

A clinker path laid in right-angle herringbone.

Repeating Unit Pattern. This pattern consists of courses that wind themselves around a central unit, forming a rectangle or square of any size. It is ideal for a decorative terrace paving or as a focal point at a junction of paths.

Diagonal Bond. This is a variation of the stretcher bond in which each brick is laid at 45 degrees to the path or terrace edge. A single row of bricks should frame the bond and act as an edging.

Herringbone. A popular bond, Herringbone is used not only in the garden but also on streets. In its classic form it consists of a repeating pattern of two bricks laid on a diagonal, meeting at 90 degrees, and producing a very stable, interlocking bond. At least one course of bricks should be laid as a base line on either side. The bond starts and ends with a specially fit half brick cut on site.

Right-angle Herringbone or Elbow Bond.
This is a further variation of the herringbone, suitable for paths or as a frieze around terraces. Instead of being laid at 45 degrees to the edge of the path it is laid at 90 degrees, so that the courses are parallel to the edge.

Basket weave, Block, and Parquet Bond.
Of all the bonds this has the most variations. The basic principle involves assembling a pattern of standard blocks made up, for example, of two bricks side by side. Adjacent blocks are turned through 90 degrees to form the pattern. Further variations include double basket weave (blocks of eight brick pavers) and half basket weave. If the pavers are laid on edge the "weave" appears to be more delicate. Different colored bricks can be used to emphasize the weaving pattern. The secret of laying the more complicated versions of this bond is to adhere strictly to the grid.

Any size area can be covered in this pattern, however the more cross joints there are the lower the load bearing capacity. This is not a bond to be hidden in the garden, rather one to be on full view.

Jack in Jack, Stack Bond or Cross Bond.
As with many other paving bonds, several names exist for this same bond, often leading to confusion. The principle characteristic of this bond is the crossed joints. Bricks are laid systematically in courses side by side; the joints line up and cross. This bond is possible with both square and rectangular

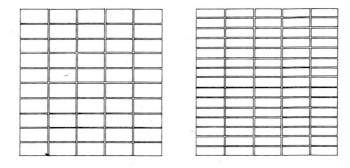

bricks, however it takes great skill to lay this bond over large areas. Any mistakes lining up the bricks will be clearly visible. Cross bond is not very stable and cannot be used for vehicular traffic. The precise appearance does work well with modern architecture.

Examples of bonding patterns illustrate how various types of brick pavers should be laid.

Top Left: When laying rectangular standardized sizes in stack (cross) bond, ensure that the bricks are laid in an exact grid. This bond is only suitable for terraces and patios that will not be driven on.

Top right: The same bond laid on edge.

Bottom: This is the recommended technique to lay a curve.

Terracotta Tiles

The warm brown surface of terracotta awakens memories of holidays in warm, tropical settings. The chance to recreate a holiday paradise in your own garden, complete with tubs of Oleander and furniture to match, is hard to resist. One important difference usually mars the realization of this dream, however: namely, the climate. The comparatively thin terracotta tiles are not so highly fired as clay brick or clinker and are therefore vulnerable to frost damage. Only tested products with a certificate of frost resistance should be considered for use.

As the majority of these pavers or tiles are handmade, they are characterized by slight variations. Larger sizes might have curled up corners, which is part of the rustic charm. They are difficult to lay, and even when laid in mortar a totally smooth tiled surface, as in a bathroom, cannot be expected.

Terracotta is generally supplied in rectangular and square formats. The smaller hexagonal or octagonal paving stones that are available are not always successful outdoors, as they can be too small and out of proportion with the area they cover. The image of country style paving, with light color differences from paver to paver, is part of the character. In combination with different surface materials, particularly pebble mosaics, very attractive designs can be created with terracotta which accentuate the southern feeling.

Above: Terracotta tiles straight out of a holiday brochure. For those who are lucky enough to have a holiday home in the south, the links between the floor covering, the edging of the pool, and the planting shown here give a good example of a successful design.

Right: The glowing honey colors of these terracotta tiles are very attractive. Unfortunately this material cannot be used in areas with severe winters.

Timber in the Garden

Timber in its many forms is a popular material in the garden. It is very versatile and may be adapted to many uses. Purchased as squared planks it can be used to create decks and platforms reminiscent of waterside. As wood chippings it produces informal woodland paths. The form and type of finish dictate how and where timber can be best used.

Preventive measures can help protect timber against rot, decay, insect and fungal attack caused by constant dampness, standing water, and general weathering. These measures include pressure impregnation or painting with timber preservative. Even with treatment continued maintenance is necessary. The use of proven environmentally friendly products is recommended, as these do not release toxins into the atmosphere or ground. Pressure treated timber, available in many building centers, should last a decade or more without follow up treatment.

Below: Wood chippings between regularly spaced grooved wooden sleepers. When choosing this type of surface you should be aware that it will eventually decay even if it has been treated.

Next page: This natural and unpretentious path shows the most organic way of using wood.

Timber modules and decks that are raised on a suitably constructed base can dry off better and thus last longer than timber that is in direct contact with the ground. Timber paving and timber decks are normally of soft native woods such as spruce, fir, pine, and larch. Tropical hardwoods should be avoided, as the advantages of teak, mahogany, bongossi, or bangkirai are outweighed by the cost to the environment. Red cedar, which is similar to the tropical hardwoods in both color and durability, is a good alternative. At the top of the list of naturally durable native woods is oak, with a lifespan of fifteen to twenty-five years, followed by douglas fir and larch with lifespans of ten to fifteen years. Spruce, fir, and pine can be expected to last five to ten years. Signs of natural weathering such as bleaching by the sun and general wear and tear are part of the character and charm of wood.

Left. The tiny narrow garden of this terrace house has been transformed into a deck landscape. The large squares form patios, the smaller ones serve as links.

Right: Timber decks awaken images of the outdoor life, of recreation, and of closer ties with nature.

Clever use of color with timber can draw separate elements together to form a whole.

Next page: Deck modules are cheap and quick to lay and are ideally suited to create patios that directly adjoin the house.

Timber Decks

Decks are closely associated with water. They evoke images of jetties, of poolside, and of lakeside decks with warm foot-friendly surfaces, welcoming after the cool water of the pool. Attractive even when unfurnished, decks are an extension of the living space with or without the obligatory swimming pool. When custom built to suit the location, even the most daring designs can be achieved - overlapping raised levels, diagonally laid planks, and overhanging projecting platforms. Through the use of holes cut to accommodate existing trees, the trees too can be incorporated into the design.

Deck planks or boards are secured to joists in a construction similar to that of a timber floor indoors. For durability, good ventilation and a well draining sand or gravel bed are essential. To minimize the danger of slipping on wet, smooth surfaces, planks should be grooved to provide better grip.

Planks can be stained to match or to contrast with the color scheme of the surroundings. For most gardens, the most successful colors are greys in all shades from light blue-grey to anthracite.

Designed specifically for this location, this deck appears at first glance to be quite simple. On closer examination, however, it is full of well thought-out details - from the cutouts for the trees to the spotlights in the floor.

Deck Modules - the Outdoor Parquet

Deck modules, or unit decking as it is often called, may be likened to a kind of outdoor parquet. This type of surface is ideal for terraces and patios. Units consist of prefabricated standard-sized square or rectangular modules made out of spruce or fir planks. They are fixed to a supporting grid or alternatively placed directly on the ground. The space between the modules should correspond to the gaps between the planks, forming their surface in order to maintain visual continuity. This may be achieved through the use of spacers between adjacent units. As a rule, one size of module is used throughout a scheme. These can be laid parallel to each other or in alternate directions to form a basket weave pattern. Depending on the supplier a variety of sizes are offered.

Railway Sleepers

As a an early example of recycling, railway sleepers found great favor with garden designers in the 1970s and were used for everything from steps and retaining walls to - of course - paving. This initial enthusiasm has since waned, primarily due to the fact that the tar with which all old sleepers were impregnated is a health hazard. However, this is no reason to dispense altogether with railways sleepers as a design element. New, pressure treated sleepers are more expensive but safer, and can be bought in a variety of section sizes in standard and special lengths. The strong lines characteristic of this material work well as paving or steps, although the surface tends to be slippery when wet.

Wood Block Paving

Squared end-grain wood blocks are perhaps best known as an indoor floor surface material in workshops. At the turn of the century, however, they were used for paving streets, urban passageways, and in between tramlines in order to reduce the noise levels. These blocks still find favor today because their regular shape complements both modern architecture as well as everyday buildings. Blocks are manufactured from pressure treated pine, spruce, or oak. Square or rectangular sawn sections are cross-cut to

make cubes or rectangular blocks. The cubes are generally available as 4 x 4 x 4 inches and 3 x 3 x 3 inches, while the rectangles have lengths of either 3 inches or 5 inches. Like bricks, they can be laid with either staggered joints or in the less stable but more decorative stack bond also known as cross bond. Edge constraint can be provided by nailing blocks together where they adjoin a soft area. Should additional edging be incorporated or a change of material planned, however, it is wise to include an expansion joint to allow for the expansion and contraction of the wood.

Log Paving

In the 1970s and early 1980s all types of timber paving were popular, particularly log paving (also known as wooden rounds, roundwood block or disc paving). These were widely featured in garden shows and probably inspired the introduction and use of concrete disc paving imitation.

Log paving is made using machine stripped softwood tree trunks which are cross-cut into billets or logs of appropriate length. Common lengths are 4 inches, 6 inches, and 8 inches. The longer the length, the longer lasting the paving. Logs are generally supplied in sections measuring 2 1/2 - 10 inches in diameter, but larger dimensions can be ordered. This timber paving can be laid using logs of a uniform diameter or, for a more lively effect, logs in a variety of sizes. Since it is in contact with the ground, the timber must be treated to ensure a longer life. Logs should have a similar moisture content to the ground in which they will be laid and should be soaked if necessary before use. Large differences in the moisture content induce cracks and accelerate rot. Before opting for this kind of paving one should consider the disadvantages, namely the slipperiness of the surface when wet, the short lifespan, and the uncompromising pattern. These factors limit its use to specific areas.

Left: Cross-cut logs used as stepping stones may become mossy and slippery; nonetheless they form a wonderful short cut through a woodland garden.

Above: Roundwood or log paving is not without its problems. In order to prolong life expectancy the logs require stable conditions without great variations between wet and dry.

Wood Chips

Used for many years as either mulch for newly planted areas or as a soft bouncy surface in children's play areas, wood chips are equally suitable for paths. Wood chips are a by-product of forestry but can also be produced from garden prunings using an organic shredder. Whatever the source, material to be used for paths should not be of too fine a texture. Ideal for curved and irregular paths, the material can provide a flowing transition into the planting. However, this tendency to spread is not always an advantage. What is desirable in a woodland setting can be a nuisance in the vegetable plot. A suitable edging, using branches or a timber board, provides a simple solution. Bark and wood chippings naturally absorb and hold water. Though this is a useful part of their function as mulch, for path material it can prove a disadvantage. Without a well drained sub-base the path can easily become a quagmire. From time to time it is also necessary to replenish the surface with fresh material. Nonetheless, these disadvantages are a small price to pay for such an environmentally sound material.

Coarse wood chippings make a woodland path par excellence.

Next page: Wood chippings are ideal in many situations, particularly in woodland, shade, or natural gardens where the emphasis lies on the planting.

Below: Not every
plant needs to be
pulled out of the
path.

Next page: Gravel is
the ideal material for
this path, providing
a light surface
between the dark
plants.

Loose Aggregates

The search to find materials suitable for pleasing, functional, yet inexpensive hard surfaces is as old as gardening itself. For the long drives, extensive network of paths, and large courtyards of stately homes the solution was loose aggregate. This consisted of a loose covering of gravel, broken stone, or hoggin (red rock) laid on a compacted hardcore base. Despite high maintenance levels these surfaces are currently experiencing a renaissance. With its unassuming character, this material lends itself equally well to old and new settings. When used in combination with other paving materials, the possibilities are nearly limitless. By choosing the appropriate type of stone, color highlights and links to the surroundings can be achieved.

Classic gravel

Gravel drives bestow an air of elegance, the ambiance of a country house. Gravel is so indispensable to the garden that one readily accepts all the concomitant disadvantages, including damage to shoes, irritating bits that find their way into the home, and the unavoidable tasks of raking and weeding. Even the magnetic attraction gravel has for small children as a medium for play is part of its charm. The characteristic crunching sound made by gravel when walked upon is an essential part of the garden experience.

In its finest and most refined form gravel is used as an ornament in paterres. This is an art form in which labyrinths of narrow paths and shapes, defined by box hedges, are picked out in different colored gravels. Such ornamental uses are not restricted to historic gardens. Given a suitable location it is feasible to break away from the restrictions imposed by the normal grey surface and adopt a color reminiscent of the Renaissance. If a product of the local quarry, gravel bought locally blends nicely into the surroundings. In addition, a great variety of exotic gravels are available offering a choice of color:

White: Carrara marble, grain size 1/4 - 5/8 inches

White-beige: Quartzite, grain size 1/8 - 5/8 inches

Red: Crushed brick, grain size 1/8 - 3/8 inches*

Yellow: Giallo Sienna or Cotswold yellow, grain size 1/8 - 3/8 inches

Black: Coal slag, grain size 1/8 - 1/4 inches*

Green-grey: Diabas split, grain size 3/8 - 1/2 inches

Grey-purple: Granite split, grain size 1/4 - 3/8 inches

(*coarse grained hoggin material)

In the construction of garden paths, the frost proof hardcore sub-base is covered with a 1 1/4 - 1 1/2 inch blinding layer of small sharp stones. This effectively fills the spaces in the top of the sub-base, without impairing

Opposite page: A classic gravel courtyard can be transformed into a sitting area. This principle may be applied to any front garden that is large enough to provide privacy.

Left: Herb gardens and gravel paths are a popular combination, the one complements the other. Here a particularly attractive golden gravel provides that extra bit of color.

Right: This formal gravel garden demonstrates a play on colors. It uses grey granite gravel in the beds, limestone gravel for the paths, and large pebbles around the trees.

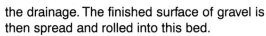

the drainage. The finished surface of gravel is then spread and rolled into this bed.

As previously stated, the level of maintenance required for gravel is prohibitive for many people. The key is to view it not as a drudgery, but as one of the many "therapeutic" garden tasks that must be carried out from time to time.

Hoggin

Although often dismissed as dusty when dry and slimy after rain, hoggin (or red rock) surfaces are nevertheless useful in landscape parks and gardens. They can even, if constructed on a sufficient base, be used for vehicular traffic. Depending on local availability, sand, limestone, crushed brick, or coal slag can be used for the surface. A literal translation of the German name "water-bound

scattered-surface" gives a good indication of the construction. The material consists of grains that are 1/8 inch in size. When wet these bind the larger stones together and by compaction, form a dense mass. The compact surface allows little water to penetrate, therefore a good camber and adequate surface drainage is essential. These, together with a properly constructed base can reduce maintenance costs considerably. Not only paths but larger open spaces can be surfaced in this

Gravel need not be restricted to paths and terraces. A dramatic impact can be created by covering the whole garden. This is an ideal solution for gardens in arid conditions.

material. The life expectancy is much less than stone and brick surfaces, but providing it is on a good base the top layer can simply be renewed when worn. Although edging may appear out of place in many settings, it is nevertheless necessary to secure and define the line of the path during construction.

Green Paths

Paths and surfaces which are not regularly used need not always be grey or brown - they can be green. The degree of greenness depends on a variety of factors described in the variations below.

Grass Paths

There is nothing more seductive than a short, cropped, mown pathway through a flower meadow. When no longer used it is recolonized by the meadow and simply disappears. It follows that the route can change at a whim to wander through any part of the garden. To establish a grass path, sow a mixture of grasses and herbs which are reasonably resistant to wear. Mow regularly to encourage growth and density. In newly sown meadows or lawns which have not yet developed a matted surface, you may be impatient for the pathways to develop. The process can be accelerated by laying down narrow strips of turf to form an instant path.

Reinforced lawns

In simple terms, this is nothing more than colonized gravel. It is a finish that can stand up to heavy wear and makes an ideal surface for occasional parking. From a distance the surface appears green. Only on closer inspection does its real construction become apparent. To develop a reinforced grass surface, simply rake a mixture of soil and grass seed into the top layer of a normally constructed gravel surface. Like all green paving, fortified grass needs time to become established before it can be used, as well as a period for regeneration after intensive use or drought.

Large granite paving stones with wide grass filled joints make this path both beautiful and fitting in this setting.

Next page: Heather gardens can appear somewhat forlorn and artificial if not properly integrated into the garden. The green lines of the grass filled joints tie the island bed to the rest of the garden and form an essential element of the overall design.

Grass Joints

In contrast to conventional paving design, this paving depends on making the joints the most dominant visual element. The green grid pushes the hard paving into the background, partially covering it and relegating it to second place. In this way the green component in a small garden can be maximized and an uninterrupted transition created between path and lawn. This variation can reconcile conflicting functional and aesthetic requirements. For example, it might be desirable to extend the grass right up to the house yet at the same time provide a solid path. The boundaries of the flower border can merge into the path or formal paving, softened by greening the joints. This idea can be applied to traditional stone or concrete slabs, paving stones, or brick pavers, provided consideration is given to the design of the joints.

The width of the joint should be visually pleasing but also wide enough to support the successful growth of grass and other plants. The joint must be in proportion to the stone size. One half-inch is suitable for small element paving stones, increasing to one inch or more for large paving stones and slabs. The lower section of the joint is filled with coarse sand or split (grit) and the upper inch is topped with soil that has been premixed with seeds.

Right: The grass area invaded the paving, thus increasing the proportion of green in the garden.

Below: A path has been mown to avoid trampling down the meadow on the way to the sitting area at the bottom of this garden. It is the contrast between the short and long grass which is so attractive. However, grass is not the best surface if the path is to be frequently used.

In the summer, fierce heat can burn the grass, leaving it brown and ugly. Frequent watering and protection from traffic during the initial stages are both vital to establish a good growth. Spontaneous colonization of little used or neglected areas of paving by grasses, herbs, or (in shaded areas) mosses is considered by some to be a nuisance. On the contrary, it can be interesting and attractive. The paving is not harmed by such growth and fastidious weeding becomes superfluous. Low growing and ground hugging herbaceous plants often find conditions in the cracks and crevices ideal and can extend adjacent flower beds into the path or patio for a quite charming effect.

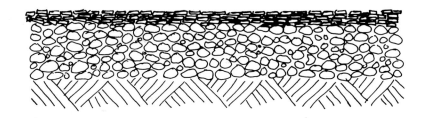

Path construction for loose aggregate surfaces and "green" surfaces with light traffic. For heavier loads use the appropriate construction (refer to page 46). If the ground is free-draining a frost protection layer is not necessary.

For wood chips:
• 2 1/2" wood chips
• 4-6" gravel or hardcore

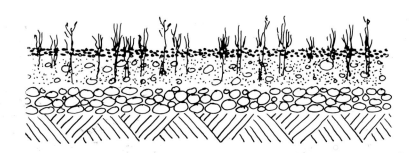

For fortified grass:
• 1 1/4" split (crushed stone) with grass seeds raked in
• 4-6" hardcore and top soil
• 4-6" gravel or hardcore
• Frost protection layer if required

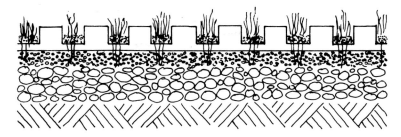

For "grasscrete" paving:
• Block paving (3-5") either concrete or brick, filled with top soil mixed with grass seeds
• 1 1/4-2" sand or split (crushed stone) bed
• 8" gravel or hardcore
• Frost protection layer if required

For a gravel or crushed stone surface:
• 3 1/8" gravel or crushed stone
• 8" gravel or hardcore
• Frost protection layer if required

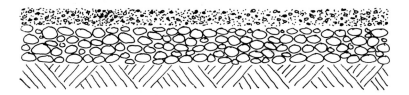

For a hoggin surface:
• 2-4" sand
• 8" gravel or hardcore
• Frost protection layer if required

Edging

Path edgings, mowing edges, and bed surroundings should be considered in the design from the beginning, rather than simply be left to chance. Where two surfaces meet there must either be a dividing line or a transitional zone. In gardens, these are not just ornamental but technical necessities. Edging holds the path together, giving it stability and preventing lateral movement and displacement. It is usually raised to form a curb; this helps keep loose material such as gravel or wood chippings in place and additionally prevents soil from spilling over onto the paving.

Edging should relate to the paving material and be appropriate for the situation. The safest and simplest option is to choose the same material throughout, however contrasts either in color or material can be interesting. Some edgings (such as rustic tree stems) relate best to a country setting, while others are not so specific and are at home anywhere. In some situations, especially natural settings, edging may be unnecessary. Woodland and grass paths which flow into their surroundings are good examples of this.

Regarding construction, edging should be laid before the paving. The finished height of the edging should be at least 2 inches higher than the adjoining surface. Edging must be secured in a concrete haunch and the joints cleanly pointed with mortar (this does not apply to rustic tree stems).

Edging can also be used to frame important specimens of plants.

Left: A course of
Carrara marble
paving stones on
either side indicates
the boundary of this
overgrown hoggin
path and provides
the necessary lateral
constraint.

Edging is rarely included in the square foot price quoted for hard surfaces. When quoted, it is generally priced by the foot. Do not forget to include this cost in the final calculation. It is not worth economizing on this essential part of the paving, as subsequent remedial work can be even more expensive. If a raised edge appears too hard and formal for the situation, a good compromise is to set the outer rows of paving in a mortar bed with mortar joints. The lateral support is thus within the hard surface itself. This edging band can also act as a drainage channel if laid in a concave form. The number of rows used depends on the size or width of the paved area and the size of the material. As a rule, an uneven number is more pleasing than an even number of rows. While suitable for paths intended for pedestrian and occasional

vehicular use, this solution is not recommended for steady vehicular traffic.

Though precise, mechanical edges look tidy, greenery should still be allowed to spill over. Part of the garden's charm is provided by the interaction between the functional barrier and the uncontrolled growth allowed to drape over the edge. Decide whether decoration, if any, should be incorporated in either the paving or the edge. Utilizing both surfaces generally produces chaos and detracts from the garden as a whole.

Bed Surroundings

Flower beds as well as paths can be edged. During the last century metal or brick ornamental edging in a variety of motifs, including acanthus leaves and lilies, was

popular. This fashion extended even to lawns, which were neatly framed to draw attention to them. Such treatment would seem overdone and fussy to our present tastes, which call for simpler forms. A single row of large paving stones or bricks on edge, for example, retains the soil yet admirably complements the planting.

Mowing Edges

Mowing edges form an integral part of an English garden and are works of art in their own right. They are functional without being showy: narrow metal strips or simple wooden battens giving the appearance of holding back the turf. Both are set a little lower than the base of the grass so as to be unobtrusive and not interrupt the line of the surface. Above all, they are practical and facilitate effective mowing; the lawn is higher than the neighboring surface, thus allowing the lawn mower to overrun the edges.

Left: When choosing an edge for mosaic paving select a stone size slightly larger than that used on the surface itself. The strong color contrast shown here between marble and granite would enrich any path.

A selection of unusual edgings all with strong visual character derived from color, shape, and form.

Left: At the turn of the century a great variety of edging was available, much of which can still be purchased on the second-hand market. A few such as "Rope Top" are being currently manufactured again by specialist firms.

Right: Flower beds can be edged as shown here, with three rows of natural stone paving stones laid in mortar. Soil is prevented from spilling onto the lawn, overhanging plants are not caught by the lawn mower, and the lawn mower can overrun the edge of the lawn without incurring damage.

Next page: Slender branches define a wood chip path. The edging should always suit both the surface and the garden style.

Next page: What at first glance appears just a uniform surface is revealed on closer inspection as a carefully laid geometric pattern of triangles and circles.

Creative Floorscapes - The Art of Pebble Mosaic

Pebble mosaics, more than any other type of paving, are the ultimate design for the garden. Whether laid like a carpet over a large area or just a single motif they are truly eye-catching. The ancient Greeks decorated their town squares with intricate designs and virtually all Mediterranean countries have developed their own indigenous forms of mosaic art. The concept of using the floor as an ornamental surface is not restricted to southern Europe, however. Old towns in Germany such as Freiburg, Goslar and Darmstadt offer magnificent examples. Church squares, thresholds, even alleyways are transformed into works of art. Geometric shapes such as diamonds, circles, ovals, and stars and patterns such as basket weave, scrolls, and arabesque decorate what would otherwise be dull, mundane surfaces. In the garden, this it the place to make a personal statement - a hand-crafted, individual design, tailored to suit the surroundings.

The best pebble sizes for creating patterns and pictures are between 1 1/2 and 3 inches in diameter. Small squared mosaic paving stones or tessera could also be used. These produce a completely different effect and require great skill in laying; they are also more expensive. Round or elongated pebbles are easier to obtain and, if the basic rules are followed, relatively simple to lay. Pebbles are shaped by the action of water over thousands of years. They are tactile and attractive and it is very tempting to collect the material yourself from beaches, riverbanks, or creeks. No one

Below: When pebbles are wet the colors come alive and are seen at their best. The design shown uses brown, blue-black, and white pebbles.

objects to the occasional stone taken as a souvenir but the larger quantities required to make a pebble mosaic are a different matter. If in doubt, check whether it is permissible to remove material. Above all, never remove anything from protected sites or conservation areas. All good paving suppliers have pebbles for sale, generally graded according to their color and size.

Pebbles can be laid flat or placed on end like closely packed eggs. The size of the joints is important. Under no circumstances should the joints dominate the design; they are there simply to hold the elements in place. The material used for the bedding and joints determines the finer aesthetics of pebble mosaic. There are basically three methods of construction to choose from, each giving a subtle variation. All are laid on a base which has been designed to take light traffic:

• The sand bed method is the most traditional. The pebbles are simply pressed into a bed of sand about 1 1/2 inches deep. When all the pebbles have been laid, or at the end of a day´s work, sand is brushed over the surface and gently washed into the joints. It is advisable to work in sections that are two feet square, progressively increasingly the size as more experience is gained.

• The mortar bed method substitutes mortar for the sand. Only as much mortar should be spread as can be completed in approximately two hours, for after this time the mortar tends to harden, making it difficult to press the pebbles into position.
Both the sand bed and the mortar bed methods employ the same technique of placing the pebbles gently in position and pressing them evenly with a long wide plank to ensure that the surface is level.

Using the smallest pebbles, graded according to size and color, it is possible to create many different designs. Unfortunately there are few craftsman who can lay such a fine frieze as this.

• The precast method enables the mosaic to be prefabricated indoors and when set hard taken to the site and placed in position. It is important to consider the shape and size of the finished mosaic and how it fits into the surroundings. Larger floorscapes can be divided like a giant jigsaw puzzle, numbered and then reassembled on site. Since the mosaic form is rigid, it is essential to ensure a good base. The construction resembles an upside-down cake, with the "fruit" being the pebbles that are carefully but tightly laid at the bottom of the mold in a layer of sand. Over this is a poured a backing of strong mortar. Only after this has set can it be removed from the mold. (For more information, refer to *Mosaik* by Peggy Vance and Celia Goodrick-Clarke).

Paving with a pebble finish suffers two disadvantages; it has a limited load carrying capacity and is therefore unsuitable for vehicular traffic, and it can be very slippery when wet. Nor does it score highly when judged solely on walking comfort, yet this is a small price to pay for such a beautiful feature in the garden.

There are many fantastic examples of pebble mosaic to be seen and found; once you have developed an eye for this craft you will find inspiration galore on which to base your own designs.

Simple patterns of pebble paving can be used not only within a larger area of pebbles but also as individual vignettes framed by other materials. Movement and tension are vital to

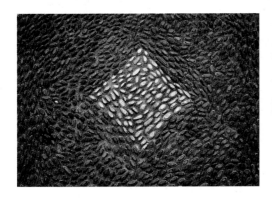 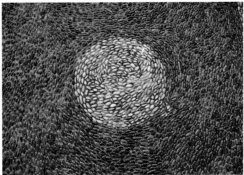 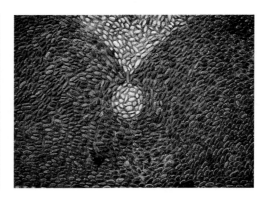

all pebble mosaics. Even when mono-chrome uniformed sized pebbles are used, much can be achieved by varying the direction in which the pebbles are laid. The dark pebbles appear to swirl around the white circle in ever decreasing rings. Small details can be particularly signifi-cant; one example is the link between the tip of the diamond and the drop.

Diameter	Name	Color	Shape
1 1/2-2 1/2"	Carrara	white, light grey	round, smooth
	Diabase	green	rounded
	Flintstone	dark grey	rounded
	Granite	grey-white speckled	rounded
	Granite	red-white speckled	rounded
	Porphyry	red/brown/greys	rounded
	Porphyry	red/brown/greys	split
	Serpentine - Gravel	green-black	sharp
3-6"	small cobbles	greys	round, smooth
	glacier stones	white-black speckled	round, smooth
	Quarzite cobbles	yellow-white	round, smooth
	Verde Nero	green-anthracite	rounded

These lustrous
ceramic spheres are
unusual and arrest-
ing.

Next page: Indi-
vidual pebble
mosaics are an ideal
medium for personal
expression in the
garden. To be fully
appreciated they
must be in a promi-
nent position and
not tucked away
from view.

A mosaic pattern must be set correctly within the surrounding surface to achieve the optimum effect. There are two possible ways to accomplish this: the mosaic can be set flush as part of the walking surface or alternatively be slightly raised, as in the snake and star designs illustrated. This has the effect of giving the mosaic a three dimensional quality. A light-dark contrast between white Carrara marble and dark granite or even basalt is the simplest to execute. The most successful examples employ a strong clear motif.

Appendix

Schroeder (Folly Farm, Edwin Lutyens); **88 top** Peter Howcroft (Lanning Roper); **88 bottom** Wolfram Stehling; **89** Arbeitsgemeinschaft Pflasterklinker; **90** Gary Rogers (Palm Beach Gardens, Schatzi Gaines); **91** Heidi Howcroft (Pippa Humphreys); **92** Ron Sutherland/GPL; **93** Brian Carter/GPL, Chelsea Flower Show 1989; **94** Ron Sutherland/GPL (Duane Paul Design Team); **95** D. Vorillon/SIP (T. Bosworth); **96** T. Jeason/SIP; **97 left** C. Sarramon/SIP (Maison J. Guillermain); **97 right** J. P. Lagarde/SIP; **98** Heidi Howcroft; **99 left** Linda Burgess/GPL (RHS Wisley, Surrey); **99 right** Gary Rogers; **100** Gary Rogers (Ulrich & Hannelore Timm, Willy Hinck); **101** Ron Sutherland/GPL, Mien Ruys Garten, Holland; **102** Gary Rogers; **103** Peter Howcroft; **104 left** Brigitte Thomas/GPL; **104/105** Gary Rogers (Rosie Young); **105** Gary Rogers (Little Morton); **106, 107** Gary Rogers (Fountain Halls, Arizona, Fran & Wally Worn); **108** Wolfram Stehling; **109** Gary Rogers (Maria Laach); **110 left** Tommy Candler/GPL; **110 right** Gary Rogers (Sir Terence Conran); **111** from Freiflachen an öffentl. Gebauden naturnah gestalten und pflegen; **112** Heidi Howcroft; **113 top** George Meister (Gottfried Hansjakob); **113 bottom** George Meister (Heidi Howcroft); **114 left** Ron Sutherland/GPL; **114/115** Ron Sutherland/GPL; **115 right** Ron Sutherland/GPL; **116 left** John Miller/GPL; **116/117 middle** George Meister; **117 right** Juliette Wade/GPL; **118** N. Millet/SIP; **119** Bernard Touillon/SIP; **120** N. Millet/SIP; **121** Heidi Howcroft; **123** Practical Gardening/Colin Leftley (Nuala Laycock, Mathew Bell for Zeneca Ltd); **124 left** Gary Rogers (Chatsworth House, Dennis Fisher); **124 right** Heidi Howcroft; **125** Gary Rogers (Chatsworth House).

GPL: Garden Picture Library, London
SIP: Stock Image Production, Paris
VGB: Vereinigte Granit Betriebe, Fürstenstein

Bibliography

The majority of the following literature which deals with paving in depth is only available in German. For those interested in the subject it is worth looking at these books for the pictures alone.

Baetzner, Alfred. *Natursteinarbeiten.* Stuttgart, Germany, 1983.

Howarth, Maggy. *The Art of Pebble Mosaics.* Tunbridge Wells, 1994.

Howcroft, Heidi. *Pflaster für Garten, Hof und Plätze.* Munich, Germany, 1994.

Informationsdienst Beton-Bauteile. *Beton-Bauteile für den Garten.* Bayern.

Klein, Renè. *Walks, Walls & Patio Floors.* Menlo Park, California: Sunset Books, 1986.

Lehn, Irmgard, bearbeiter. *Historisches Pflaster.* Denkmalschutz in Darmstadt. Darmstadt o. J.

Mehling, Günther, ed. *Natursteinlexikon.* Munich. Germany, 1993.

Nickl, Peter, and Heidi Howcroft, ed. *Die Kunst des Pflasterns.* Exhibition catalogue: Munich, Germany, 1985.

Timm, Ulrich. *Terrassen und Sitzplätze.* Munich, Germany, 1995.

Vance, Peggy, and Celia Goodrick-Clarke. *Mosaik.* London, England, 1994.

Wolff, Heinz. *Das Pflaster in Geschichte und Gegenwart.* Munich, Germany, 1987.

Ziegelforum. *Ziegel-Lexikon.* Munich, Germany, 1988.

Ziegler, Max. *Fachkunde für Strassenbauer.* Munich, Germany, 1978.